Musk's Vision

Musk's Vision

Guiding Tesla's Future Success

Mack Rafeal

UNIEK ENTERPRISES

CONTENTS

INDEX

Introduction

In the domain of visionary business people, hardly any figures stand as unmistakably as Elon Musk. A nonconformist with an uncanny capacity to combine mechanical development with a persistent quest for aggressive objectives, Musk has become inseparable from pivotal endeavors that challenge the tried and true way of thinking. At the front line of this confounding business person's portfolio is Tesla, an organization that has re-imagined the car business as well as made way for a more extensive change of the energy and transportation areas.

Elon Musk's excursion with Tesla is a story of boldness and conviction, energized by a dream that reaches out a long ways past the limits of conventional plans of action. From the origin of Tesla Engines in 2003 to the current day, Musk's unfaltering obligation to supportability, development, and a future fueled by clean energy has been the directing power impelling the organization to remarkable levels. This presentation digs into the complexities of Musk's vision for Tesla, investigating the key components that have molded the organization's direction and inspecting the groundbreaking effect it has had on ventures that were once considered impenetrable to change.

Vital to Musk's vision for Tesla is the idea of maintainable transportation. Well before "green" and "electric" became trendy expressions in the auto business, Musk saw the potential for electric vehicles (EVs) to upset individual transportation. With a firm conviction that feasible energy arrangements were urgent for the planet's future, Musk set off on a mission to make an organization that wouldn't just deliver electric vehicles however would likewise rethink the manner in which individuals see and connect with cars.

Tesla's presentation vehicle, the Roadster, denoted a change in perspective in the car scene. An all-electric games vehicle, the Roadster broke assumptions about the capacities of electric vehicles. Musk showed the way that electric vehicles could be both superior execution and harmless to the ecosystem, testing the overall incredulity encompassing the achievability of electric drive. The progress of the Roadster established the groundwork for Tesla's ensuing endeavors, giving the monetary and mechanical catalyst expected to seek after Musk's more stupendous vision.

As Tesla's process unfurled, Musk's vision developed past simply delivering electric vehicles. He imagined an exhaustive biological system that would coordinate feasible energy age, energy capacity, and transportation. The presentation of the Tesla Powerwall, Powerpack, and Megapack denoted the organization's introduction to energy capacity, permitting buyers and organizations to proficiently bridle and store environmentally friendly power. This comprehensive way to deal with energy arrangements situated Tesla as a vital participant in the car area as well as in the more extensive change toward a manageable and decentralized energy lattice.

A crucial second in Tesla's direction accompanied the presentation of the Model S, an extravagance car that not just exhibited the exhibition capacities of electric vehicles yet additionally displayed Musk's obligation to feel and plan. The Model S's smooth and moderate plan tested conventional thoughts of what an electric vehicle could be, making manageability inseparable from complexity. The progress of the Model S not just cemented Tesla's situation in the auto market yet additionally pushed Musk's vision into the standard, enamoring buyers and industry specialists the same.

Be that as it may, Musk's vision for Tesla stretches out past the domain of buyer vehicles. A striking declaration in 2015 presented the Tesla End-all strategy, Part Deux, framing Musk's aggressive guide for the organization's future. This plan included extending Tesla's product offering to incorporate electric trucks, transports, and the critical Model 3, a more reasonable electric vehicle pointed toward making economical transportation open to a more extensive segment. Musk's obligation to mass-market electric vehicles addressed a change in outlook, testing the thought that ecological cognizance ought to come at a higher cost than expected.

The divulging of the Tesla Model 3 out of 2017 denoted a turning point for the organization. With its moderately reasonable price tag and great reach, the Model 3 made exceptional progress, turning into the smash hit electric vehicle worldwide and breaking misinterpretations about the market's hunger for electric vehicles. Musk's vision of carrying reasonable transportation to the majority was emerging, and Tesla's impact started to reach out a long ways past the car area.

Essential to Musk's vision is the affirmation that a reasonable future requires something beyond jolting the car armada. The progress to clean energy should be exhaustive, tending to each part of energy utilization. This acknowledgment prompted Tesla's endeavor into sun oriented energy arrangements with the securing of SolarCity in 2016. Musk imagined a future where each home and business could outfit sunlight based power, further decreasing reliance on non-renewable energy sources. The combination of sun powered energy with Tesla's energy stockpiling items made a synergistic environment that enabled customers to produce, store, and use their own spotless energy.

Tesla's obligation to maintainability isn't exclusively restricted to its items however stretches out to the assembling system also. Musk has underscored the significance of making a shut circle, supportable energy framework, where the energy utilized in assembling Tesla vehicles is obtained from sustainable sources. Gigafactories, decisively situated all over the planet, assume a significant part in accomplishing this objective. These monstrous creation offices smooth out assembling processes as well as integrate environmentally friendly power arrangements, making them basic parts of Musk's more extensive vision for a practical future.

The worldwide effect of Musk's vision for Tesla is maybe most obvious in the organization's job in speeding up the progress to electric portability. As customary automakers wrestle with the difficulties of zap, Tesla has arisen as a pioneer, setting the benchmark for electric vehicle execution, range, and charging framework. Musk's procedure of zeroing in on very good quality, superior execution vehicles at first has shown to be an essential masterstroke, permitting Tesla to put resources into innovation and foundation that has therefore sifted down to additional reasonable models.

The outcome of Tesla has not been without its portion of difficulties and contentions. Musk's unfiltered correspondence style, described by productive utilization of virtual entertainment, has sometimes landed him in steaming hot water. From public debates with administrative specialists to feature snatching occurrences, Musk's way of behaving has, on occasion, eclipsed the surprising accomplishments of Tesla. However, it is definitively Musk's flighty methodology and ability to face challenges that have impelled Tesla to the very front of development.

One of the most troublesome components of Musk's vision is the idea of independence. Musk imagines a future where Tesla vehicles are electric as well as completely independent, fit for exploring without human intercession. The sending of cutting edge driver-help frameworks, like Tesla's Autopilot, addresses a venturing stone toward this aggressive objective. While the quest for full independence has confronted administrative investigation and innovative difficulties, Musk stays unfazed, stressing the potential for independent vehicles to change transportation and decrease mishaps.

Past the domain of earthly transportation, Musk's vision stretches out to the universe. SpaceX, one more endeavor under Musk's umbrella, intends to make humankind a multi-planetary animal groups. The interaction among SpaceX and Tesla is in excess of a simple occurrence; it addresses Musk's all encompassing way to deal with tending to the difficulties confronting humankind. While SpaceX centers around the investigation and colonization of different planets, Tesla tries to make Earth more maintainable, making a harmonious relationship that lines up with Musk's general vision for the fate of humankind.

Musk's vision for Tesla isn't bound to the short term; it stretches out to the drawn out supportability of the planet. Environmental change and ecological debasement are existential dangers that request earnest consideration and inventive arrangements. Musk sees Tesla as an auto and energy organization as well as an impetus for a more extensive shift toward a feasible and tough future. The organization's statement of purpose epitomizes this vision, expressing its obligation to speeding up the world's change to manageable energy.

The effect of Musk's vision isn't restricted to the progress of Tesla as an organization; it reverberates with a worldwide development toward supportability and clean energy. Tesla's accomplishments have prodded conventional automakers to speed up their electric vehicle drives, states to put resources into charging framework, and customers to embrace the possibility of electric portability.

Musk's capacity to motivate change reaches out past the meeting room; it penetrates cultural insights and standards, rocking the boat and encouraging an aggregate shift toward a more manageable future.

Taking everything into account, Elon Musk's vision for Tesla rises above the ordinary limits of business system. It is an outline for a future where manageability, development, and human inventiveness combine to address the squeezing difficulties confronting mankind. From electric vehicles to environmentally friendly power arrangements, independence to space investigation, Musk's vision is an embroidery of brassy objectives woven together by a tireless quest for a superior, more feasible world. As Tesla proceeds to develop and rethink ventures, Elon Musk's vision fills in as a directing light, enlightening a way toward a future where the limits of what is conceivable are ceaselessly pushed, and where the quest for progress is inseparable from the quest for a superior, more economical future for all.

1. **Setting the Stage: The Rise of Elon Musk**
   Elon Musk's brilliant ascent from a somewhat obscure business person to quite possibly of the most persuasive figure in the business and innovation areas is a story woven with daringness, development, and a tireless quest for extraordinary objectives. Brought into the world in Pretoria, South Africa, in 1971, Musk's initial interest with innovation and business foreshadowed a vocation that would reclassify ventures and push the limits of what was considered conceivable.
   Musk's process started enthusiastically for figuring and innovation, clear since early on. His pioneering soul surfaced in his teen years when he established a computer game programming organization called Zip2. Sent off in 1996, Zip2 expected to give online professional references and guides to papers, a dream that was relatively radical. Albeit the underlying years were set apart by monetary battles and distrust from conventional news sources, Musk's persistence paid off when Compaq obtained Zip2 in 1999 for almost $300 million. This early achievement set up for Musk's resulting adventures and gave him the monetary establishment to seek after additional aggressive undertakings.
   The bonus from the offer of Zip2 filled in as the capital for Musk's next adventure, X.com, a web-based installment organization. In 2000, X.com converged with Confinity, an organization established by Peter Thiel and Max Levchin, and the subsequent substance ultimately became known as PayPal. Under Musk's administration, PayPal arose as a prevailing player in the blossoming field of online installments. The organization's prosperity pulled in the consideration

of industry goliaths, prompting its obtaining by eBay in 2002 for $1.5 billion. Musk, presently a multimillionaire, might have settled for the status quo, however his desires arrived at a long ways past web-based installments.

Elon Musk's introduction to the aeronautic trade started with the foundation of SpaceX in 2002. Energized by a dream of making space investigation more open and supportable, Musk established SpaceX determined to lessen space transportation costs and in the long run colonizing Mars. The improvement of the Hawk 1, SpaceX's most memorable orbital rocket, was met with beginning misfortunes, remembering a bombed send off for 2006. Nonetheless, the ensuing effective send off of the Hawk 1 out of 2008 denoted a memorable second, making SpaceX the main secretly financed organization to arrive at circle.

Around a similar time, Musk put his focus on an industry that appeared to be impenetrable to change: car. In 2004, Musk joined Tesla Engines, an electric vehicle startup established by Martin Eberhard and Marc Tarpenning. Seeing the potential for electric vehicles to rethink the car scene, Musk put vigorously in Tesla and turned into its biggest investor. By 2008, Musk played assumed the part of President and item planner, directing the organization toward a future where feasible transportation was a specialty market as well as a worldwide objective.

The monetary emergency of 2008 represented a huge test for Tesla. With the auto business faltering from monetary slumps, doubters scrutinized the suitability of a startup zeroed in on electric vehicles. Musk confronted an impressive errand of controlling Tesla through monetary disturbance while at the same time pushing the limits of electric vehicle innovation. The presentation of the Tesla Roadster in 2008 denoted a critical second, showing the way that electric vehicles could be superior execution, upscale, and attractive.

While Tesla was getting some decent forward momentum in the car world, SpaceX kept on arriving at new achievements in space investigation. The fruitful send off of the Bird of prey 9 rocket in 2010 cemented SpaceX's situation as a key part in the aeronautic trade. Musk's double job as President of Tesla and SpaceX displayed his capacity to at the same time oversee mind boggling, high-risk adventures. The equals between his electric vehicle and space investigation tries highlighted Musk's general vision for a reasonable future that stretched out past the limits of our planet.

As Tesla picked up speed, it confronted difficulties that went past monetary requirements. Incredulity about the possibility of electric vehicles, worries about battery innovation, and the absence of charging foundation presented huge snags. Musk, be that as it may, stayed undaunted. His public picture turned out to be progressively inseparable from boldness and perseverance, as he utilized his own image to reinforce trust in Tesla and its central goal. The divulging of the Model S in 2012 denoted a defining moment, laying out Tesla as an amazing powerhouse in the car business.

The progress of the Model S exhibited the abilities of electric vehicles as well as displayed Musk's obligation to plan and advancement. The smooth, moderate tasteful of Tesla's vehicles tested conventional ideas of what electric vehicles could be, situating manageability as a component instead of a split the difference.

The honors and grants gathered by the Model S highlighted Musk's capacity to combine natural cognizance with buyer allure, an accomplishment that had evaded numerous in the auto business.

The ensuing presentation of the Model X, an all-electric SUV with unmistakable bird of prey wing entryways, and the more reasonable Model 3 showed Musk's obligation to extending Tesla's product offering. The Model 3, specifically, meant to carry manageable transportation to a more extensive crowd by offering a more reasonable electric vehicle with mass-market claim. The uncovering of the Model 3 of every 2017 denoted a turning point for Tesla, with extraordinary interest and a creation increase that highlighted the developing craving for electric vehicles.

In the midst of Tesla's prosperity, Musk's public persona turned out to be progressively captivated. His unfiltered correspondence style via web-based entertainment, joined with his penchant for taking on strong enemies, prompted both esteem and analysis. From public questions with administrative specialists to feature getting episodes, Musk's conduct frequently eclipsed the noteworthy accomplishments of Tesla. However, it is exactly this unconventional methodology that has added to Musk's notable status, depicting him as a nonconformist business visionary unafraid to rock the boat.

Past electric vehicles, Musk's vision for Tesla stretched out to energy arrangements. The securing of SolarCity in 2016 denoted an essential move to coordinate sun powered energy into Tesla's biological system. Musk imagined a future where each home and business could produce, store, and utilize its own spotless energy. The presentation of the Tesla Powerwall, Powerpack, and Megapack further hardened Tesla's part in the progress to economical energy arrangements, making a comprehensive environment that tended to transportation as well as the more extensive test of energy utilization.

The improvement of Gigafactories all over the planet turned into a foundation of Musk's technique for accomplishing maintainability. These enormous creation offices smoothed out the assembling system as well as consolidated environmentally friendly power arrangements. Musk imagined these Gigafactories as something other than assembling plants; they were fundamental parts of a shut circle, practical energy framework that lined up with his more extensive vision for a perfect and decentralized energy network.

Musk's obligation to supportability stretched out past Tesla's items and assembling processes. He underscored the significance of changing the world to sustainable power sources, for natural reasons as well as for monetary and international security. Musk's support for a carbon-impartial future and his contribution in different natural drives highlighted his faith in the pressing requirement for worldwide activity to address environmental change.

A focal principle of Musk's vision is the quest for independence in transportation. The presentation of Tesla's Autopilot and Full Self-Driving (FSD) capacities denoted a huge move toward understanding Musk's objective of accomplishing completely independent vehicles. While the turn of events and sending of independent driving innovation have confronted administrative difficulties and periodic misfortunes, Musk stays unfaltering in his conviction that self-driving vehicles will upset transportation, making it more secure, more proficient, and eventually prompting a critical decrease in mishaps.

Musk's vision for Tesla isn't restricted to Earth. His interest with space investigation and the colonization of Mars prompted the foundation of SpaceX. The transaction among SpaceX and Tesla isn't unintentional; it mirrors Musk's comprehensive way to deal with tending to the difficulties confronting humankind. While Tesla centers around economical answers for Earth, SpaceX expects to make mankind a multi-planetary animal categories. The cooperative energy between these endeavors exemplifies Musk's brassy vision for the eventual fate of humankind.

All in all, the ascent of Elon Musk and the climb of Tesla address a change in outlook in the business and innovation scene. Musk's excursion from a youthful business visionary intensely for innovation to the Chief of numerous noteworthy organizations highlights his capacity to mix development, desire, and strength. The story of Tesla's development, directed by Musk's vision, is a demonstration of the groundbreaking force of pioneering soul and the quest for daring objectives. As Tesla keeps on reclassifying businesses and challenge standards, Elon Musk remains as an image of the dauntless soul that pushes mankind toward a future where maintainability, development, and the tireless quest for progress unite to make a superior world for all.

2. Overview of Tesla's Journey in Sustainable Innovation

Tesla's excursion in manageable development is a story of desire, disturbance, and an immovable obligation to reshaping businesses. From its initial days as an electric vehicle (EV) startup to its flow status as a worldwide innovator in reasonable energy arrangements, Tesla's development under the direction of Elon Musk has been set apart by a constant quest for historic innovations and a dream for a more economical future.

The commencement of Tesla Engines in 2003 denoted the start of another time in auto history. Helped to establish by Martin Eberhard and Marc Tarpenning, the organization meant to rock the boat of fuel controlled vehicles by presenting superior execution electric vehicles. In any case, it was Elon Musk's entrance into the scene, as a financial backer and possible President in 2008, that catalyzed Tesla's change into a power that would rethink the car business as well as the more extensive scene of economical development.

Fundamental to Tesla's process is its obligation to electric vehicles as an impetus for a cleaner, more feasible transportation biological system. In the mid 2000s, the predominant discernment was that electric vehicles were restricted to little, unreasonable plans with deficient reach.

Tesla looked to challenge this discernment with the arrival of the Tesla Roadster in 2008. This all-electric games vehicle, in view of the Lotus Elise undercarriage, not just broken assumptions about electric vehicle execution yet additionally showed the way that maintainability could coincide with top of the line, elite execution cars.

The progress of the Roadster gave the energy and monetary assets for Tesla to seek after its more extensive mission: making electric vehicles standard. The disclosing of the Model S in 2012 denoted a defining moment in Tesla's excursion. An all-electric extravagance vehicle, the Model S exhibited Tesla's obligation to plan, execution, and reach. Its smooth feel, state of the art innovation, and noteworthy reach moved conventional automakers to reconsider their way to deal with electric portability.

One of the basic components that put Tesla aside was its emphasis on building a biological system instead of simply producing vehicles. The Supercharger organization, a quick charging foundation for Tesla vehicles, addressed a huge hindrance to electric vehicle reception — the worry about charging openness and speed. By decisively conveying Supercharger stations, Tesla planned to make really long travel in electric vehicles as helpful as conventional fuel controlled vehicles, a significant stage in the organization's main goal to change the world to practical transportation.

The ensuing presentation of the Model X, an all-electric SUV with unmistakable bird of prey wing entryways, and the more reasonable Model 3 further extended Tesla's scope. The Model 3, specifically, expected to carry electric vehicles to the majority by offering a more reasonable choice without settling on reach and execution. The reaction to the Model 3 was overpowering, with uncommon interest and creation challenges that highlighted the craving for economical transportation on a worldwide scale.

While the auto area was the underlying concentration, Tesla's excursion in reasonable advancement stretched out past electric vehicles. The obtaining of SolarCity in 2016 denoted an essential move into the sunlight based energy area. Elon Musk imagined a coordinated methodology where Tesla's energy items, electric vehicles, and sunlight based arrangements would frame a harmonious environment. The Tesla Powerwall, Powerpack, and Megapack, combined with sunlight based chargers, expected to make a shut circle framework where buyers could create, store, and utilize their own spotless energy.

The Gigafactory idea became instrumental in Tesla's excursion toward maintainability. These monstrous creation offices, decisively situated all over the planet, not just worked with the proficient assembling of Tesla vehicles and energy items yet additionally assumed a pivotal part in accomplishing Musk's vision of a maintainable future. Gigafactories were planned for scale as well as to consolidate environmentally friendly power sources, making them basic to Tesla's central goal of progressing the world to supportable energy.

The Gigafactory in Nevada, known as Gigafactory 1, turned into a point of convergence for Tesla's battery creation. The improvement of the Gigafactory was tied in with expanding creation limit as well as about driving down the expense of batteries — a vital consider making electric vehicles more reasonable. The Gigafactory model has since been duplicated worldwide, with Gigafactories in Shanghai and Berlin further setting Tesla's situation as a forerunner in feasible development on a worldwide scale.

Tesla's process likewise saw the improvement of Autopilot, a high level driver-help framework that planned to carry independent driving capacities to Tesla vehicles. While the idea of self-driving vehicles confronted administrative investigation and innovative difficulties, Autopilot addressed a stage toward Musk's vision of completely independent vehicles. The quest for independence was about accommodation as well as about security, with the conviction that cutting-edge driver-help frameworks could essentially decrease mishaps and save lives.

Tesla's introduction to the energy area and its accentuation on making a maintainable energy biological system were underlined by Musk's "Ground breaking strategy." Uncovered in 2006 and refreshed in 2016, the All-inclusive strategy illustrated Musk's vision for Tesla's future, enveloping the improvement of many electric vehicles, sun powered items, energy capacity arrangements, and independent driving innovation. The Ground breaking strategy filled in as a guide for Tesla's development, directing the organization's endeavors to reform both the auto and energy businesses.

The effect of Tesla's maintainable development reaches out past its immediate items and advancements. The organization's prosperity has resonated through the auto business, prodding conventional automakers to speed up their electric vehicle drives. The "Tesla impact" has tested industry standards, demonstrating that electric vehicles can be attractive, high-performing, and economically fruitful. This shift has had flowing impacts on the whole inventory network, from battery makers to charging foundation suppliers, making a far reaching influence of development and change.

Tesla's impact has stretched out to the monetary business sectors too. The organization's financial exchange execution has been out and out uncommon, with Tesla becoming one of the most important automakers around the world. The enthusiasm around Tesla's stock has filled the organization's monetary strength as well as featured the developing financial backer interest in practical and imaginative organizations. Tesla's outcome in the monetary business sectors has situated it as an image of the crossing point between maintainability, innovation, and monetary practicality.

In spite of its accomplishments, Tesla has not been safe to difficulties and discussions. Musk's whimsical correspondence style, his collaborations via online entertainment, and periodic spats with administrative specialists have created titles.

From public debates with the Protections and Trade Commission (SEC) to provocative articulations on Twitter, Musk's way of behaving has, now and again, eclipsed the organization's accomplishments. Nonetheless, the contentions have not essentially hosed Tesla's direction, and Musk's irregular methodology has turned into an indispensable piece of the organization's story.

Looking forward, Tesla's excursion in manageable advancement keeps on developing. The organization's emphasis on propelling battery innovation, the improvement of new vehicle models, and its venture into new business sectors exhibit a pledge to continuous development. The declaration of the Cybertruck, Tesla's all-electric pickup truck, and the aggressive objectives framed in the End-all strategy Part Deux highlight Musk's unflinching vision for Tesla's future.

Chapter 1

The Visionary Mindset

The visionary outlook is a mental methodology described by a singular's capacity to think past the customary limits of current conditions and imagine a future that rises above existing constraints. A psychological system powers development, cultivates imagination, and pushes people toward pivotal accomplishments. The individuals who have a visionary mentality are many times driven by a profound feeling of direction, an enthusiasm for change, and a guarantee to having an enduring effect on the world.

At its center, the visionary outlook includes a change in context - a takeoff from business as usual and a readiness to challenge the standards. Visionaries view difficulties as any open doors, misfortunes as illustrations, and the obscure as a domain ready for investigation. This mentality enables people to embrace vulnerability and explore uncertainty with a feeling of interest as opposed to fear.

One of the vital qualities of a visionary mentality is the capacity to see associations and examples that might escape others. Visionaries have an all encompassing perspective on the world, perceiving the complicated exchange of different factors and understanding the potential expanding influences of their activities. This interconnected reasoning permits visionaries to expect patterns, distinguish arising amazing open doors, and devise thorough answers for complex issues.

Besides, the visionary outlook is intently attached to areas of strength for an of direction. Visionaries are driven by a convincing longing to contribute definitively to society, whether through mechanical progressions, social change, or social development. This feeling of direction goes about as a directing power, giving guidance and inspiration during seasons of vulnerability or difficulty.

Development is a sign of the visionary outlook. Visionaries continually look to push the limits of what is conceivable, testing the standard way of thinking and investigating unfamiliar regions. This quest for development frequently implies an eagerness to face challenges and embrace disappointment as a fundamental piece of the educational experience. Visionaries comprehend that disappointment isn't a barrier but instead a venturing stone on the way to progress.

The visionary attitude isn't restricted to a particular industry or field; it very well may be tracked down in the domains of science, innovation, workmanship, business, and then some. Eminent visionaries since the beginning of time have shown the groundbreaking force of this mentality. People like Steve Occupations, Elon Musk, Marie Curie, and Martin Luther Ruler Jr. represent the visionary mentality through their capacity to imagine an alternate future and their tenacious quest for that vision.

One of the main traits of visionaries is their capacity to rouse and prepare others toward a shared objective. Through compelling correspondence and a magnetic presence, visionaries can revitalize people and networks to go along with them on their excursion. This ability to fabricate an aggregate vision is especially clear in developments for social change, where visionary pioneers light a common feeling of direction and responsibility among their devotees.

Training assumes an essential part in supporting and developing the visionary outlook. Conventional school systems frequently underscore similarity and adherence to laid out standards, which can smother the imaginative reasoning fundamental for a visionary mentality to flourish. Notwithstanding, inventive instructive methodologies that empower decisive reasoning, interest, and investigation can give fruitful ground to the advancement of visionary reasoning.

Notwithstanding instruction, openness to different encounters and viewpoints can essentially add to the improvement of a visionary outlook. Travel, cooperation with people from various foundations, and commitment with different disciplines expand one's perspective and cultivate a more exhaustive comprehension of the interconnectedness of thoughts and frameworks.

The visionary outlook is definitely not a static characteristic however a powerful quality that develops after some time. It requires consistent learning, variation, and an eagerness to embrace change. Visionaries are not limited by unbending philosophies but rather are available to rethinking their convictions and techniques in light of new data and developing conditions.

In the business world, the visionary attitude is frequently connected with fruitful business venture. Business people with a visionary mentality are not exclusively persuaded by monetary benefit but rather are driven by an enthusiasm to make something new and effective. They see potential open doors where others see difficulties, and their endeavors are directed by a drawn out vision as opposed to transient increases.

Besides, the visionary attitude stretches out past the person to impact hierarchical societies. Organizations that cultivate a culture of development and urge workers to think innovatively are bound to adjust to changing economic situations and remain in front of the opposition. In such associations, workers are enabled to contribute their thoughts, go ahead with carefully weighed out courses of action, and seek after aggressive objectives.

The crossing point of innovation and the visionary mentality has prompted the absolute most huge progressions in late history. Developments in man-made reasoning, biotechnology, environmentally friendly power, and space investigation are driven by people who have a visionary mentality. These visionaries influence innovation as a device to carry their plans to completion, making answers for complex issues and molding the fate of mankind.

Be that as it may, the visionary mentality isn't without its difficulties. Visionaries frequently face doubt, protection from change, and the innate vulnerability related with graphing new ways. Keeping up with versatility notwithstanding difficulty is a critical part of the visionary outlook. The capacity to endure through difficulties, gain from disappointments, and adjust to unanticipated conditions is fundamental for transforming a visionary thought into a substantial reality.

Moral contemplations likewise assume a critical part in the turn of events and utilization of the visionary outlook. As people endeavor to rejuvenate their dreams, they should explore the moral ramifications of their activities. Mindful development includes considering the likely outcomes of mechanical headways, guaranteeing that progress lines up with moral standards, and moderating any adverse consequences on people and society.

The visionary attitude isn't restricted to fantastic, world-evolving thoughts; it can appear in regular day to day existence through little demonstrations of imagination and advancement. Whether it's tracking down a more productive method for getting done with a responsibility, acquainting a clever methodology with critical thinking, or rocking the boat in a specific space, the visionary mentality can be developed in different settings.

All in all, the visionary outlook is a strong power that pushes people and social orders toward progress and development. It includes a takeoff from regular reasoning, a guarantee to a higher reason, and a persevering quest for extraordinary thoughts. Visionaries can see associations, expect drifts, and move others to go along with them on their excursion.

The improvement of the visionary mentality requires a blend of schooling, various encounters, and a readiness to embrace change. In a world that is continually developing, the visionary outlook isn't simply a mentality yet a guide to molding a superior future for all.

1.1. Elon Musk's Vision for a Sustainable Future

Elon Musk, a visionary business person and Chief of various weighty organizations, has become inseparable from development and a persevering quest for a supportable future. Musk's vision stretches out past individual achievement, zeroing in on changing enterprises and tending to worldwide difficulties. This paper investigates Elon Musk's vision for a practical future, looking at the critical drives and tasks he has embraced to reshape the manner in which we live and communicate with our current circumstance.

At the very front of Musk's undertakings is his obligation to progressing the world to reasonable energy. As the President of Tesla, Musk has committed significant assets to the turn of events and large scale manufacturing of electric vehicles (EVs). Tesla's main goal isn't just to make superior execution electric vehicles however to speed up the world's change to feasible energy. Musk imagines a future where sustainable power sources power our vehicles as well as our homes and organizations.

The effect of Tesla on the car business couldn't possibly be more significant. Musk disturbed the customary auto scene by demonstrating that electric vehicles could be both sleek and high-performing. The progress of Tesla's electric vehicles, like the Model S, Model 3, Model X, and Model Y, plays had a critical impact in testing assumptions about electric versatility. Musk's vision for economical transportation reaches out past private vehicles; he imagines an exhaustive shift to electric transports, trucks, and even planes.

Notwithstanding electric vehicles, Musk has focused on altering energy stockpiling. Tesla's Powerwall, Powerpack, and Megapack are energy stockpiling arrangements intended to tackle and store sustainable power for sometime in the future. These items add to the dependability of electrical lattices, work with the joining of environmentally friendly power sources, and give reinforcement power during blackouts. Musk will probably make a supportable energy environment where clean power isn't just produced yet in addition put away proficiently for steady and dependable use.

The Gigafactories laid out by Tesla assume a vital part in Musk's vision for practical energy. These monstrous assembling offices are devoted to the creation of electric vehicles, batteries, and sun based items at scale. Musk's methodology includes expanding creation limit as well as lessening costs through economies of scale. The Gigafactories are vital to making maintainable energy items more available to the overall population, facilitating the reception of clean advancements.

Past Tesla, Musk has assumed the test of changing our energy framework through SolarCity, a sun oriented energy administrations organization. Obtained by Tesla in 2016, SolarCity centers around sunlight based energy age and capacity answers for private, business, and modern applications. By coordinating sun oriented innovation with energy capacity frameworks, Musk expects to make a circulated and strong energy network that lessens reliance on conventional matrix frameworks controlled by petroleum derivatives.

Musk's advantage in space investigation isn't just about extending human presence past Earth; it is likewise profoundly associated with his vision for a manageable future. As the pioneer and President of SpaceX, Musk is pursuing making humankind a multi-planetary animal types. The reasoning behind this aggressive objective is established in the idea of planetary overt repetitiveness - guaranteeing the endurance of the human species by laying out a presence on other heavenly bodies.

SpaceX's Starship, a completely reusable space apparatus presently being developed, is integral to Musk's vision of making life interplanetary. Musk imagines Starship not just as a vehicle for ran missions to Mars yet for the purpose of empowering fast and savvy travel between Earth, the Moon, and different objections in the planetary group. By decreasing the expense of room travel, Musk intends to make it financially possible for people and enterprises to investigate and use assets past our home planet.

The use of room assets is a critical part of Musk's vision for manageability. Space rock mining, an idea Musk has supported, includes extricating significant minerals and assets from space rocks to fulfill the rising need for unrefined components. By taking advantage of the tremendous assets of room, Musk imagines a future where Earth's limited assets are enhanced by those accessible in the more extensive planetary group, diminishing the ecological effect of asset extraction on our planet.

Musk's advantage in space isn't restricted to the potential for asset extraction; it additionally integrates with his interests about Earth's weakness to existential dangers. Musk has been vocal about the requirement for mankind to turn into a multi-planetary animal groups as a protect against horrendous occasions, like space rock influences or other planetary-scale fiascos. The colonization of Mars, as per Musk, is a proactive measure to guarantee the drawn out endurance of the human species.

While Musk's vision for a practical future envelops aggressive tasks like Tesla and SpaceX, it likewise stretches out to tending to perhaps of humankind's most squeezing challenge - environmental change. Musk has reliably upheld for atrocity to alleviate the effect of environmental change and plays underlined the part of maintainable energy in lessening fossil fuel byproducts. He accepts that changing to sustainable power sources isn't just an ecological goal yet additionally a basic step for the drawn out prosperity of our planet.

Notwithstanding his work with Tesla and SpaceX, Musk has been engaged with different drives pointed toward tending to environmental change. One outstanding model is the Musk Establishment's contribution in the XPRIZE Carbon Expulsion rivalry. Musk promised a significant award handbag to energize inventive answers for eliminating carbon dioxide from the air, featuring his obligation to supporting and boosting endeavors to battle environmental change.

Musk's promotion for a feasible future goes past his job as a business chief; it stretches out to impacting popular assessment and strategy. Through stages like Twitter, Musk shares his viewpoints on sustainable power, environmental change, and the significance of progressing away from non renewable energy sources. His dynamic commitment via web-based entertainment has made him an unmistakable voice in the public talk on ecological issues, adding to expanded mindfulness and conversations around economical practices.

While Musk's vision for a supportable future is unquestionably aggressive and sweeping, it isn't without its faultfinders. A contend that Musk's way to deal with supportability is driven more by mechanical good faith than a far reaching comprehension of the financial and political variables that add to ecological difficulties. Others question the achievability of Musk's interplanetary colonization vision, refering to the massive specialized, calculated, and moral difficulties related with such undertakings.

Also, concerns have been raised about the natural effect of specific parts of Musk's endeavors. For instance, the development of electric vehicle batteries, notwithstanding being a basic part of the change to feasible transportation, includes mining and handling materials with natural outcomes. Musk has recognized these provokes and has communicated a pledge to tending to them, underlining the requirement for constant improvement and development in manageable practices.

Pundits have additionally directed out the potential for Musk's endeavors toward intensify social imbalances. The significant expense of Tesla's electric vehicles, for example, restricts their openness to more affluent people. Musk's emphasis on space investigation, while catching the creative mind of many, has been condemned for redirecting assets from additional prompt and major problems on The planet, like neediness, disparity, and medical services.

In light of such reactions, Musk has safeguarded his methodology, stressing the requirement for advancement and financial suitability to drive boundless reception of supportable advances. He contends that by making electric vehicles optimistic and high-performing, Tesla can impact the more extensive car market and speed up the shift towards feasible transportation. Additionally, Musk sees the monetary outcome of SpaceX as fundamental for financing aggressive undertakings like the improvement of Starship and the colonization of Mars.

Musk's double job as a visionary business person and individual of note has made him a polarizing figure. While celebrated for his commitments to innovation, development, and manageability, he has additionally confronted examination for his correspondence style, which now and again has been disputable and unfiltered. Musk's associations via web-based entertainment, especially Twitter, have prompted both deference and analysis, with some adulating his realism and others communicating worry about the possible effect on monetary business sectors and public discernment.

All in all, Elon Musk's vision for a manageable future envelops a large number of drives, from upsetting the car business with electric vehicles to laying out a human presence on Mars. His work with Tesla, SpaceX, and different endeavors mirrors a promise to tending to worldwide difficulties, including environmental change, asset shortage, and the requirement for planetary overt repetitiveness. While Musk's methodology has gathered far and wide consideration and backing, it isn't without doubters and pundits question the practicality, morals, and more extensive ramifications of his aggressive vision. No matter what one's position, there is no denying Musk's effect on molding the discussion around maintainability and pushing the limits of what is viewed as conceivable in the domains of innovation, space investigation, and natural stewardship.

1.2. The Driving Force Behind Tesla's Success

Tesla, the electric vehicle (EV) and clean energy organization, has arisen as a groundbreaking power in the car business and then some. At the core of Tesla's prosperity is a blend of visionary initiative, mechanical development, and a promise to manageability. This exposition investigates the main thrust behind Tesla's prosperity, diving into the key factors that have moved the organization to the front of the electric vehicle market and situated it as a forerunner in the more extensive domain of clean energy.

Visionary Initiative:

One of the essential drivers of Tesla's prosperity is the visionary initiative of its fellow benefactor and President, Elon Musk. Musk's vision reaches out past only making electric vehicles; it incorporates an extensive change of the car business and a pledge to supportable energy. Musk's capacity to explain a convincing vision and his persevering quest for aggressive objectives have been instrumental in molding Tesla's direction.

Musk's vision for Tesla goes past the customary perspective on an automaker. He imagines a future where electric vehicles are functional as well as alluring, contending with and outperforming their gas powered motor partners regarding execution, plan, and reasonableness. This vision rocks the boat and rethinks the assumptions related with electric versatility.

Moreover, Musk's initiative style is described by an involved methodology and an eagerness to face huge challenges. His contribution in the specialized and designing parts of Tesla's items is obvious, and he frequently pushes the limits of customary reasoning.

Musk's nervy objectives, like the large scale manufacturing of reasonable electric vehicles and the colonization of Mars through SpaceX, have become inseparable from his authority style and add to Tesla's picture as an industry disruptor.

Mechanical Development:

At the center of Tesla's prosperity is its persevering obligation to mechanical advancement. Tesla's electric vehicles are not just utilitarian options in contrast to conventional vehicles; they address a change in outlook in auto innovation. The organization's attention on creating state of the art electric drivetrains, battery innovation, and independent driving abilities has separate it in the serious scene.

Tesla's development in battery innovation is especially critical. The organization's utilization of lithium-particle batteries with high energy thickness has considered expanded range and further developed execution in its electric vehicles. The improvement of the Gigafactory, a gigantic office devoted to battery creation, has empowered Tesla to increase creation and decrease costs, making electric vehicles more open to a more extensive market.

Independent driving innovation is another region where Tesla has taken huge steps. The presentation of Autopilot, Tesla's semi-independent driving element, and Full Self-Driving (FSD) capacities exhibit the organization's obligation to propelling the fate of transportation. While FSD isn't completely understood and faces administrative difficulties, Tesla's steady updates and upgrades grandstand its commitment to pushing the limits of independent driving.

Tesla's accentuation on over-the-air programming refreshes is a novel part of its way to deal with development. This component permits Tesla to consistently improve and upgrade its vehicles' exhibition, usefulness, and wellbeing without requiring actual mediations. This unique way to deal with programming refreshes lines up with the high speed nature of mechanical progressions and guarantees that Tesla proprietors benefit from the most recent elements and enhancements.

Shopper Allure:

Tesla's prosperity isn't exclusively ascribed to mechanical development; it likewise relies on the allure of its items to customers. Tesla has figured out how to make electric vehicles alluring by consolidating execution, plan, and supportability. The smooth and modern plan of Tesla's vehicles, combined with their noteworthy speed increase and reach, has tested predispositions about electric vehicles being dull or unfeasible.

The Tesla Model S, presented in 2012, assumed a critical part in changing discernments about electric vehicles. With its striking plan, elite execution, and long reach, the Model S showed the way that electric vehicles could be both harmless to the ecosystem and exciting to drive. Ensuing models, including the Model 3, Model X, and Model Y, have extended Tesla's item setup, taking care of various market sections and inclinations.

The Supercharger organization, Tesla's restrictive quick charging framework, addresses a huge concern related with electric vehicles - range tension. The far and wide accessibility of Superchargers permits Tesla proprietors to attempt really long travel with the affirmation of quick and advantageous charging. This framework has added to the reception of electric vehicles by reducing worries about the common sense of long excursions.

Tesla's immediate to-purchaser deals model is another element that separates it in the auto business. By bypassing customary showroom organizations, Tesla have some control over the client experience, give nitty gritty data about its items, and smooth out the buying system. This approach lines up with the organization's ethos of testing laid out standards and embracing a more straightforward and straightforward relationship with buyers.

Market Interruption and Industry Impact:

Tesla's prosperity isn't bound to its effect on the electric vehicle market; it stretches out to the more extensive auto industry. The organization's problematic presence has provoked laid out automakers to speed up their endeavors in electric vehicle advancement. Tesla's prosperity fills in as both an impetus for development and a benchmark against which different automakers measure their advancement in the electric vehicle space.

The charm of Tesla's prosperity has additionally reached out to the monetary business sectors. The organization's stock presentation has been a subject of critical conversation and investigation. The taking off valuation of Tesla, making it one of the most significant automakers all around the world, reflects financial backer trust in the organization's vision, administration, and potential for future development. Nonetheless, it has likewise prompted banters about market elements, valuation measurements, and the maintainability of such securities exchange patterns.

Tesla's effect on the auto business goes past electric vehicles. The organization's way to deal with over-the-air refreshes, direct deals, and accentuation on client experience has incited conventional automakers to reconsider their systems and embrace parts of Tesla's plan of action. The effect of Tesla's prosperity is clear in the rising spotlight on electric vehicles by heritage automakers, as they endeavor to rival the Silicon Valley upstart in the developing auto scene.

Natural Stewardship:

A focal fundamental of Tesla's central goal is ecological maintainability. Past assembling electric vehicles, the organization is focused on lessening its generally speaking ecological effect. Tesla's joining of sustainable power sources in its tasks, like sunlight based chargers and energy stockpiling arrangements, lines up with its objective of making a shut circle energy framework.

The obtaining of SolarCity, a sunlight based energy administrations organization, in 2016 further supported Tesla's obligation to clean energy. The joining of sun oriented innovation with energy capacity arrangements empowers Tesla to offer an exhaustive set-up of items for both individual buyers and organizations. This broadening into clean energy lines up with Musk's all-encompassing vision of changing the world to practical energy sources.

Tesla's introduction to energy capacity is exemplified side-effects like the Powerwall, Powerpack, and Megapack. These energy stockpiling arrangements are intended to store power produced from sustainable sources, like sunlight based chargers, for sometime in the future. The organization of these items adds to network strength, works with the reconciliation of irregular environmentally friendly power, and gives reinforcement power during lattice blackouts.

Besides, Tesla's emphasis on energy productivity reaches out to its vehicle fabricating process. The Gigafactories, where Tesla produces electric vehicles and batteries, integrate energy-effective advancements and economical practices. The accentuation on decreasing the carbon impression of assembling lines up with Tesla's more extensive obligation to natural stewardship.

Difficulties and Reactions:

While Tesla's prosperity is certain, the organization has confronted its reasonable part of difficulties and reactions. Creation challenges, quality control issues, and worries about working environment conditions have been raised throughout the long term. The quick speed of development, while a strength, has likewise prompted periodic misfortunes and obstacles in gathering creation targets.

Tesla's Autopilot and Full Self-Driving (FSD) highlights have been the subject of investigation and debate. Pundits contend that the promoting of these elements as "Full Self-Driving" can make a misguided feeling of safety among drivers and might be untimely given the present status of independent driving innovation. The administrative scene encompassing independent vehicles adds an extra layer of intricacy and vulnerability.

The instability of Tesla's stock, while intelligent of financial backer excitement, has likewise been a wellspring of concern. A few monetary experts question the maintainability of Tesla's valuation and express wariness about the potential for market redresses. The speculative idea of the securities exchange, joined with the impact of web-based entertainment and public opinion, adds a component of flightiness to Tesla's monetary account.

Ecological contemplations connected with the extraction of natural substances for electric vehicle batteries, like lithium, cobalt, and nickel, have raised moral worries.

The mining and handling of these materials can have natural and social outcomes, featuring the requirement for dependable obtaining rehearses inside the electric vehicle industry. Tesla has recognized these provokes and communicated a guarantee to tending to them through manageable practices.

Tesla's immediate to-shopper deals model has confronted resistance in certain purviews with existing showroom regulations. Conventional showroom networks contend that Tesla's methodology upsets the laid out auto retail model and makes a lopsided battleground. These fights in court highlight the protection from change inside the auto business and the more extensive financial biological system.

All in all, the main thrust behind Tesla's prosperity is a diverse blend of visionary authority, mechanical development, purchaser request, market disturbance, industry impact, and ecological stewardship. Elon Musk's vision for a maintainable future, combined with Tesla's obligation to pushing the limits of innovation, has situated the organization as an extraordinary power in the auto and clean energy areas. While confronting difficulties and reactions, Tesla's effect on the business and its capacity to reclassify assumptions have set its status as a forerunner chasing an additional feasible and jolted future.

Chapter 2

Disrupting the Auto Industry

The vehicle business, a foundation of present day transportation, has been going through a significant change lately. Interruption, driven by innovative headways, changing buyer inclinations, and natural worries, has turned into a characterizing element of this once-steady area. From electric vehicles (EVs) to independent driving innovation, the customary car scene is being reshaped, testing laid out standards and compelling industry players to adjust or take a chance with out of date quality.

At the very front of this interruption is the ascent of electric vehicles. With worries about environmental change and a developing consciousness of the ecological effect of customary ignition motor vehicles, there has been a deliberate work to progress towards cleaner and more reasonable transportation arrangements. Electric vehicles, controlled by batteries or power modules, have gotten forward movement as a practical option in contrast to customary gas powered motors.

Significant automakers, once inseparable from the thunder of motors and exhaust vapor, are presently putting vigorously in electric vehicle innovation. Tesla, a trailblazer in the electric vehicle market, plays had a urgent impact in forming the business' direction. The organization's prosperity has not just shown the market potential for electric vehicles however has likewise provoked customary automakers to speed up their own electric vehicle advancement endeavors.

In any case, the shift to electric vehicles isn't without its difficulties. The foundation for electric vehicle charging stays a huge bottleneck. While headways are being made, the far reaching accessibility of quick charging stations is fundamental for mass reception. Legislatures and confidential substances are putting resources into charging framework, intending to make a consistent and helpful experience for electric vehicle proprietors. Conquering range tension and guaranteeing a strong charging organization will be basic for the proceeded with development of the electric vehicle market.

Notwithstanding jolt, the car business is encountering an upheaval in independent driving innovation. The possibility of self-driving vehicles has caught the creative mind of the two buyers and industry specialists. Organizations like Waymo, an auxiliary of Letter set Inc., and customary automakers are putting vigorously in the improvement of independent vehicles. The commitment of expanded security, further developed traffic stream, and improved versatility for people with restricted transportation choices has energized the competition to carry independent vehicles to the standard.

Notwithstanding, the way to completely independent vehicles is full of specialized, administrative, and moral difficulties. Guaranteeing the wellbeing of self-driving vehicles in perplexing and dynamic conditions stays a huge obstacle. In addition, administrative structures should be laid out to administer the organization of independent vehicles on open streets. The moral contemplations encompassing dynamic calculations in circumstances where living souls are in question add one more layer of intricacy to the advancement of independent driving innovation.

As the car business wrestles with the difficulties and open doors introduced by charge and independence, another problematic power is reshaping how vehicles are possessed and worked - the ascent of portability administrations. Ride-hailing stages like Uber and Lyft have changed metropolitan transportation, giving advantageous options in contrast to conventional cabs and public travel. The idea of vehicle possession is developing, with a rising number of individuals selecting on-request versatility arrangements instead of claiming a vehicle.

This change in purchaser conduct is impacting the way in which automakers approach their plans of action. A few customary producers are investigating organizations with ride-hailing organizations, while others are fostering their own versatility stages. The accentuation is presently not exclusively on selling vehicles yet on giving exhaustive transportation arrangements that incorporate a scope of portability administrations.

The reconciliation of innovation in vehicles has additionally led to the idea of associated vehicles. Current vehicles are outfitted with cutting edge sensors, correspondence modules, and infotainment frameworks that empower network with the web and different vehicles.

This network improves the driving experience as well as opens up additional opportunities for information assortment and investigation. Automakers are utilizing this information to further develop vehicle execution, give prescient support, and improve security highlights.

In any case, the expanded availability of vehicles likewise raises worries about online protection. As vehicles become more dependent on programming and correspondence organizations, they become powerless to hacking and other digital dangers. Getting associated vehicles and guaranteeing the protection of client information are foremost difficulties that the car business should address to acquire and keep up with shopper trust in this new period of car innovation.

The conventional auto production network is likewise going through a change. The shift towards electric vehicles has prompted an expanded interest for batteries and electric drivetrain parts. Thus, there is a developing spotlight on the turn of events and creation of battery innovations. Organizations work in battery assembling and materials are becoming vital participants in the car environment.

Besides, the push for manageability has prompted a reconsideration of materials and assembling processes. The vehicle business is investigating lightweight materials, like carbon fiber and aluminum, to further develop eco-friendliness and diminish natural effect. Also, the reception of 3D imprinting in the assembling system is giving additional opportunities to making complex and tweaked vehicle parts.

The disturbance in the vehicle business stretches out past the item level to how organizations are coordinated and worked. Customary automakers are confronting contest from one another as well as from new participants as tech organizations. Silicon Valley monsters like Apple and Google have communicated interest in the auto area, offering their skill in programming and computerized reasoning that would be useful.

This combination of the car and innovation enterprises has led to the idea of the "associated vehicle" and has sped up the improvement of in-vehicle infotainment frameworks, high level driver-help frameworks (ADAS), and other brilliant elements. The joint effort between customary automakers and tech organizations is obscuring the lines between the two enterprises, prompting a more unique and cooperative biological system.

The customary showroom model is likewise being tested by digitalization. Online deals stages and direct-to-shopper models are building up some decent momentum, permitting clients to sidestep the conventional showroom experience. Automakers are putting resources into online deals channels, giving clients the choice to design, buy, and even money their vehicles from the solace of their homes. This shift towards computerized retailing is reshaping the connection among automakers and shoppers, placing more control and accommodation in the possession of the purchasers.

Be that as it may, the disturbance in the vehicle business isn't without its doubters. Conservatives contend that the accentuation on electric vehicles and independence might be untimely, taking into account the current framework challenges, the ecological effect of battery creation, and the moral worries encompassing self-driving innovation. The discussion over the fate of gas powered motors versus electric vehicles, and the cultural ramifications of a completely independent transportation framework, keeps on being a subject of warmed conversation.

All in all, the vehicle business is amidst a groundbreaking period, set apart by exceptional mechanical progressions and moving purchaser assumptions. The ascent of electric vehicles, independent driving innovation, portability benefits, and associated vehicles is reshaping the customary car scene. The business' reaction to these disturbances will decide its future direction, with flexibility and advancement being the vital drivers of achievement. As the car business explores this time of progress, obviously the state of affairs is as of now not reasonable, and the people who neglect to embrace the advancing worldview risk being abandoned in the rearview reflection of progress.

2.1. Electric Vehicles as a Paradigm Shift

Electric vehicles (EVs) have arisen as a progressive power in the car business, denoting a change in outlook that reaches out past the domain of transportation. The progress from customary gas powered motor vehicles to electrically controlled options addresses a seismic change with sweeping ramifications for the climate, energy foundation, and the car environment.

At the center of the electric vehicle insurgency is a guarantee to supportability and a takeoff from the dependence on non-renewable energy sources. Conventional vehicles, fueled by gas or diesel, have for quite some time been related with natural worries, including air contamination and ozone harming substance emanations. The inescapable reception of electric vehicles presents a practical answer for relieve these ecological difficulties and move towards a more manageable future.

One of the essential benefits of electric vehicles is their diminished ecological effect. Dissimilar to gas powered motors that consume petroleum derivatives and delivery unsafe poisons, electric vehicles work with zero tailpipe emanations. This further develops air quality in metropolitan conditions as well as adds to worldwide endeavors to battle environmental change. The shift to electric vehicles lines up with the more extensive objectives of diminishing fossil fuel byproducts and progressing towards a low-carbon economy.

Vital to the outcome of electric vehicles is the headway of battery innovation. Batteries act as the energy stockpiling units for electric vehicles, fueling electric engines that drive the wheels. Throughout the long term, huge steps have been made in battery innovation, prompting upgrades in energy thickness, charging pace, and in general execution.

The improvement of lithium-particle batteries, specifically, plays had a crucial impact in making electric vehicles more commonsense and open for shoppers.

The reach uneasiness that once tormented electric vehicles, restricting their enticement for buyers, has been consistently lightened with headways in battery innovation. Current electric vehicles brag longer ranges, empowering drivers to cover significant distances on a solitary charge. As the framework for charging stations keeps on extending, worries about running out of battery power are lessening, adding to the developing acknowledgment of electric vehicles among customers.

Legislatures and policymakers all over the planet are perceiving the natural advantages of electric vehicles and executing measures to boost their reception. Motivating forces, for example, tax breaks, discounts, and sponsorships intend to make electric vehicles more reasonable and appealing to customers. Moreover, administrative drives, including outflow principles and zero-discharge vehicle commands, are pushing automakers to speed up their progress to electric vehicles and put resources into maintainable transportation arrangements.

The auto business, customarily established in the burning motor, is encountering a significant change as it turns towards electric vehicles. Laid out automakers are realigning their methodologies and making significant interests in electric vehicle advancement. Tesla, the pioneer in the electric vehicle market, has exhibited the market potential and purchaser interest for electric vehicles, provoking customary automakers to heighten their endeavors here.

While the shift to electric vehicles addresses a positive step towards ecological manageability, it likewise presents difficulties and requires a reconsideration of the current car foundation. The improvement of a vigorous charging foundation is pivotal for the broad reception of electric vehicles. Legislatures and confidential substances are attempting to grow the organization of charging stations, zeroing in on key areas like metropolitan habitats, roadways, and local locations.

Charging framework comes in different structures, going from ordinary home chargers to fast open charging stations. Home charging arrangements give accommodation to electric vehicle proprietors, permitting them to charge their vehicles shortterm. Public charging stations, then again, take care of the requirements of drivers on longer excursions, offering quicker charging rates to limit margin time. The essential situation and openness of charging foundation assume a crucial part in tending to go tension and advancing the reasonableness of electric vehicles for ordinary use.

The incorporation of brilliant innovation into charging foundation further upgrades the client experience. Versatile applications and associated frameworks empower clients to find accessible charging stations, screen charging headway, and even make installments flawlessly.

This network adds to the general comfort and openness of electric vehicle charging, building up the reasonability of electric vehicles as a viable transportation arrangement.

Past individual possession, electric vehicles are acquiring unmistakable quality in armada the executives and business applications. Organizations are perceiving the functional and natural advantages of integrating electric vehicles into their armadas. The lower working expenses, decreased support necessities, and positive ecological effect make electric vehicles an appealing suggestion for organizations hoping to line up with maintainability objectives and streamline their transportation coordinated factors.

The electric vehicle upheaval isn't bound to traveler vehicles alone; it reaches out to different methods of transportation, including transports, trucks, and, surprisingly, bikes. Electric transports are progressively being embraced in open transportation frameworks, offering a calmer and cleaner option in contrast to conventional diesel transports. Electric trucks, with their capability to reform cargo transport, are acquiring consideration from strategies organizations expecting to diminish their carbon impression.

The reception of electric bikes, like electric bikes and bikes, is filling in metropolitan conditions where brief distance driving is predominant. These minimal and energy-proficient vehicles give an economical option in contrast to conventional internal combustion bikes and cruisers. The enhancement of electric vehicles across different transportation areas highlights their flexibility and potential to reshape the whole versatility scene.

As electric vehicles become more pervasive, their effect stretches out to the energy area, affecting power age, dissemination, and utilization designs. The expanded interest for power to drive electric vehicles requires an essential way to deal with energy framework. Sustainable power sources, for example, sun oriented and wind power, are acquiring importance as the need might have arisen to charge electric vehicles.

The idea of vehicle-to-network (V2G) innovation further hazy spots the lines among transportation and energy frameworks. V2G innovation permits electric vehicles to draw power from the network as well as get overabundance energy once again to it. This bidirectional progression of energy can possibly balance out the lattice, streamline energy dissemination, and add to a stronger and practical energy environment.

The electric vehicle unrest is additionally driving developments in car plan and assembling. Electric vehicles, with their streamlined drivetrains and nonappearance of mind boggling gas powered motor parts, offer additional opportunities for vehicle design. Originators and specialists have the adaptability to rethink the design of electric vehicles, streamlining space, further developing streamlined features, and improving by and large productivity.

The shift to electric vehicles has started a reexamination of materials and assembling processes inside the car business. Lightweight materials, including carbon fiber and aluminum, are acquiring conspicuousness to further develop the energy proficiency and scope of electric vehicles. Moreover, the reception of 3D imprinting in assembling considers more noteworthy adaptability in making multifaceted and modified parts, further pushing the limits of car plan.

The union of electric vehicles with arising advancements, like man-made brain-power (computer based intelligence) and the Web of Things (IoT), is leading to the idea of savvy electric vehicles. These vehicles are outfitted with cutting edge sensors, cameras, and network includes that empower continuous information assortment and investigation. Man-made intelligence calculations improve vehicle independence, empowering elements like high level driver-help frameworks (ADAS) and prescient support.

The availability of electric vehicles stretches out past their singular abilities to envelop vehicle-to-vehicle (V2V) correspondence and vehicle-to-foundation (V2I) incorporation. This interconnected biological system works with the trading of data among vehicles and their environmental elements, adding to further developed traffic stream, upgraded wellbeing, and a more productive transportation organization.

Notwithstanding the evident advancement and capability of electric vehicles, challenges stay on the way to boundless reception. The underlying expense of electric vehicles, principally credited to the significant expense of batteries, has been a hindrance for certain customers. While motivating forces and endowments expect to resolve this issue, further decreases in battery costs through mechanical headways and economies of scale are fundamental for make electric vehicles more open to a more extensive market.

The restricted accessibility of charging foundation in specific locales represents a test to the boundless reception of electric vehicles. Resolving this issue requires cooperative endeavors from legislatures, confidential area partners, and the energy business to guarantee a thorough and very much disseminated charging organization. Public mindfulness and instruction crusades are likewise essential to disperse fantasies and confusions encompassing electric vehicles and advance their advantages.

The ecological effect of battery creation and removal is another viewpoint that requires cautious thought. While electric vehicles add to decreased emanations during their functional life, the extraction and handling of unrefined components for batteries, as well as the reusing or removal of batteries toward the finish of their life cycle, present ecological difficulties. Reasonable practices in battery assembling and reusing are basic to limit the generally speaking natural impression of electric vehicles.

The electric vehicle upset has worldwide ramifications, with various locales confronting special difficulties and amazing open doors. In created economies, where the framework for electric vehicles is further developed, the emphasis is on speeding up reception and conquering administrative obstacles. In arising economies, the accentuation is on building the vital framework, tending to reasonableness concerns, and jumping to supportable transportation arrangements.

All in all, the ascent of electric vehicles addresses a change in perspective that rises above the auto business, impacting ecological supportability, energy frameworks, and metropolitan portability. The progress from gas powered motors to electrically controlled vehicles isn't simply an innovative development yet a major reconsidering of transportation and its effect on the world. As electric vehicles keep on getting forward momentum, the cooperative endeavors of states, ventures, and buyers will assume a critical part in molding a future where manageable and productive transportation is the standard as opposed to the exemption.

2.2. Musk's Influence on Redefining Performance and Desirability

Elon Musk, a visionary business person and the main impetus behind organizations like Tesla, SpaceX, and Neuralink, has obviously made a permanent imprint on the scene of innovation, transportation, and space investigation. Among Musk's various endeavors, his effect on the car business through Tesla, Inc. stands apart as a demonstration of his capacity to rethink execution and attractiveness in the domain of electric vehicles (EVs).

Tesla, established in 2003, meant to speed up the world's progress to feasible energy through the creation of electric vehicles and sustainable power items. Under Musk's initiative, Tesla developed from a specialty player in the auto market to an imposing power that tested and upset well established shows. The progress of Tesla exhibited the feasibility of electric vehicles as well as reclassified buyer assumptions about execution, plan, and ecological awareness.

One of Musk's crucial commitments to the auto business is Tesla's attention on making elite execution electric vehicles. Generally, electric vehicles were seen as sluggish, restricted in range, and without the elating driving experience related with their gas powered motor partners. Musk looked to scatter these ideas by designing electric vehicles that matched as well as frequently surpassed the presentation of conventional games vehicles.

The presentation of the Tesla Roadster in 2008 denoted a change in outlook. Dissimilar to past electric vehicles that were frequently viewed as compromises as far as execution, the Roadster flaunted speed increase and speed tantamount to, on the off chance that not outperforming, top of the line sports vehicles. This was a turning point for electric vehicles, testing the generalization that they were inseparable from laziness. Musk's essential choice to begin with a superior presentation sports vehicle showed the way that electric vehicles could be exciting, testing the actual meaning of what an electric vehicle could accomplish.

Expanding on the outcome of the Roadster, Tesla kept on pushing the limits of electric vehicle execution with the Model S, an extravagance car that joined speed, reach, and state of the art innovation. The Model S exhibited the abilities of electric powertrains as well as broken assumptions about the restrictions of electric vehicles. Its smooth plan, Ridiculous Mode speed increase, and long-range capacities situated the Model S as a real rival in the extravagance vehicle market, interesting to a more extensive crowd past ecologically cognizant customers.

The attention on execution stretched out to the Model X and Model 3, extending Tesla's market reach. The Model X, an all-electric SUV, consolidated the common sense of a SUV with the superior exhibition ascribes of Tesla's electric powertrain. In the mean time, the Model 3 planned to make electric vehicles more open to the mass market, offering a convincing mix of execution, reach, and reasonableness. Musk's system of beginning with very good quality, superior execution models and continuously moving towards additional reasonable choices showed a sharp comprehension of market elements and purchaser inclinations.

Past execution, Musk perceived the significance of configuration in forming customer impression of electric vehicles. All things considered, electric vehicles were frequently connected with sub-par plans, looking like celebrated golf trucks. Musk looked to split away from this generalization by focusing on smooth and present day feel. The accentuation on plan spoke to purchasers' tasteful sensibilities as well as tested the idea that electric vehicles needed to forfeit style for supportability.

The moderate and modern plan language took on by Tesla turned into a sign of the brand. The shortfall of a customary grille, the smooth lines, and the moderate insides put Tesla vehicles aside in a market soaked with traditional vehicle plans. Musk's obligation to feel went past superficial contemplations; it turned into an explanation that electric vehicles could be both naturally cognizant and outwardly engaging, really testing the insight that supportability came at the expense of style.

As well as rethinking execution and plan, Musk utilized innovation to improve the allure of Tesla vehicles. The presentation of over-the-air programming refreshes permitted Tesla to constantly improve and add elements to its vehicles post-buy. This unique way to deal with vehicle refreshes upgraded the proprietorship experience as well as tested the customary model of static vehicle includes that stayed unaltered after buy.

Autopilot, Tesla's semi-independent driving component, exemplified Musk's obligation to pushing the mechanical envelope. While discussion and administrative examination went with the rollout of Autopilot, its presentation denoted a huge step towards independent driving capacities. Musk's faithful confidence in the groundbreaking capability of self-driving innovation exhibited his ability to face challenges and challenge laid out standards, even despite suspicion.

Past the domain of electric vehicles, Musk's impact reached out to the aeronautic trade through SpaceX. SpaceX, established in 2002 determined to decrease space transportation costs and empowering the colonization of Mars, accomplished historic achievements under Musk's authority. The advancement of the Hawk 9 rocket and the Mythical serpent shuttle exhibited Musk's obligation to propelling space investigation innovation.

One of SpaceX's most eminent achievements was the fruitful landing and reusability of the Hawk 9's most memorable stage. This accomplishment addressed a change in perspective in the financial matters of room travel, making it more savvy by reusing the most costly part of the rocket. Musk's accentuation on reusability and cost decrease tested customary aviation works on, preparing for another period of room investigation portrayed by expanded availability and supportability.

The aggressive objective of colonizing Mars, verbalized by Musk, gathered critical consideration and powered public interest in space investigation. Musk's vision of making mankind a multi-planetary animal categories, while met with wariness by some, highlighted his ability to think past ordinary limits. The daringness of the Mars colonization plan rocked the boat of room investigation, pushing the limits of what was viewed as achievable in the aeronautic trade.

Notwithstanding Tesla and SpaceX, Musk's impact reached out to the domain of neuroscience through Neuralink. Neuralink, established in 2016, planned to foster mind machine interface (BMI) advancements fully intent on empowering direct correspondence between the human cerebrum and outside gadgets. Musk's contribution in Neuralink exhibited his advantage in pushing the limits of innovation and investigating creative answers for address complex difficulties.

The idea of cerebrum machine interfaces, while speculative and morally nuanced, exhibited Musk's obligation to investigating groundbreaking innovations with the possibility to rethink human capacities. Musk imagined a future where people could consistently cooperate with PCs and man-made brainpower through direct brain interfaces, testing ordinary thoughts of human-machine collaboration.

Musk's effect on reclassifying execution and attractiveness stretched out past his particular dares to the more extensive tech and business biological system. His enterprising way of thinking, portrayed by a persistent quest for development, risk-taking, and an eagerness to challenge laid out standards, filled in as a motivation for another age of business visionaries and pioneers. Musk's public persona, set apart by his magnetic and frequently unfiltered correspondence style, added an interesting aspect to his impact, making him a polarizing yet irrefutably effective figure.

Nonetheless, Musk's methodology and administration style were not without discussion. His straightforward nature via web-based entertainment, public proclamations that occasionally needed traditional corporate restriction, and conflicts with administrative specialists welcomed investigation. The public picture of Musk as a nonconformist business person with an inclination for striking cases and unfiltered correspondence added intricacy to his impact, creating both esteem and doubt.

The social effect of Musk's endeavors stretched out to the more extensive discussion about the job of innovation in forming what's to come. Musk's undertakings tested assumptions about the limits of electric vehicles, the conceivable outcomes of room investigation, and the capability of cerebrum machine interfaces. His impact reverberated in the particular ventures he entered as well as in catalyzing a more extensive exchange about the extraordinary force of innovation and its suggestions for society.

The peculiarity of "Muskmania," described by an intense public interest in Musk's endeavors, was a demonstration of his capacity to catch the creative mind of individuals around the world. Musk's utilization of virtual entertainment stages, especially Twitter, as an immediate correspondence channel with people in general added to the persona encompassing his persona. The mix of visionary objectives, bold plans, and a real internet based presence made a one of a kind brand of public commitment that put Musk aside from conventional corporate pioneers.

While Musk's impact has been groundbreaking, it has not been without difficulties and debates. The dynamic and developing nature of the enterprises he entered, combined with his irregular authority style, prompted changes in open discernment. From fights in court with administrative specialists to public debates with pundits and partners, Musk's process has been set apart by snapshots of disturbance.

The impact of Musk on rethinking execution and allure reached out to the monetary business sectors. Tesla's valuation, described by critical unpredictability, reflected both the potential and dangers related with Musk's endeavors. The organization's stock cost turned into an indicator for feeling in regards to the eventual fate of electric vehicles, environmentally friendly power, and Musk's capacity to follow through on his aggressive commitments. The rollercoaster idea of Tesla's stock mirrored the market's reaction to Musk's vision, methodology, and the execution of his arrangements.

Looking forward, Musk's impact is ready to keep molding the direction of the businesses he has entered. The continuous improvement of Tesla's Cybertruck and the Roadster, SpaceX's aggressive designs for interplanetary travel, and Neuralink's quest for mind machine interface advances are demonstrative of Musk's enduring obligation to pushing the limits of what is viewed as conceivable.

The drawn out effect of Musk's endeavors on electric vehicles, space investigation, and neuroscience will unfurl over the long run, impacting ventures as well as cultural insights and assumptions.

All in all, Elon Musk's effect on rethinking execution and attractiveness in the auto business, especially through Tesla, is a diverse story of development, risk-taking, and groundbreaking vision. Musk's capacity to challenge laid out standards, reform ventures, and catch the public creative mind has made him a conspicuous and polarizing figure in the domains of innovation, transportation, and space investigation. While his methodology and initiative style have ignited contentions, there is no denying the enduring effect Musk has had on molding the fate of electric vehicles and then some.

Elon Musk, the dissident business person and visionary behind Tesla, SpaceX, and different endeavors, has unquestionably made a permanent imprint on the car and innovation enterprises. Musk's impact on reclassifying execution and attractiveness in the auto area is especially obvious through his administration at Tesla, an organization that has upset customary standards and set new guidelines for electric vehicles (EVs).

Tesla, under Musk's direction, has changed the impression of electric vehicles from being specialty, earth cognizant options in contrast to standard, elite execution vehicles. Musk's intense vision to speed up the world's progress to economical energy has been a main impetus behind Tesla's tenacious quest for development, pushing the limits of what electric vehicles can accomplish.

One of the vital components of Musk's effect on execution in the auto business is Tesla's attention on electric drivetrains. Musk perceived from the get-go that presentation was a urgent figure changing public impression of EVs. The presentation of the Tesla Roadster in 2008 denoted a defining moment, displaying that electric vehicles could be harmless to the ecosystem as well as superior execution machines. The Roadster's speed increase and maximum velocity tested assumptions, demonstrating that electric vehicles could rival, and even beat, their interior ignition partners.

Expanding on the progress of the Roadster, Musk and Tesla proceeded to foster a setup of vehicles that re-imagined the assumptions for execution in the car world. The Model S, an extravagance car, set new norms for speed increase and reach, showing the way that electric vehicles could be both down to earth for ordinary use and exciting to drive. The Outrageous Mode, presented in the Model S, became inseparable from mind-twisting speed increase, exhibiting the capability of electric powertrains to convey unrivaled execution.

Musk's impact on attractiveness is intently attached to Tesla's obligation to style, innovation, and client experience. Not at all like conventional automakers, Tesla embraced a moderate plan theory for its vehicles' insides, including huge touchscreen shows and modern style.

The smooth and present day plans of Tesla vehicles, combined with cutting edge autopilot highlights, added to the charm of claiming a Tesla past its natural advantages.

The presentation of over-the-air programming refreshes additionally accentuated Musk's obligation to ceaseless improvement and client fulfillment. Tesla proprietors experienced upgrades in execution, new highlights, and even changes in the vehicle's appearance through programming refreshes, making a feeling of expectation and fervor. This approach improved the allure of Tesla vehicles as well as tested the customary thought of a vehicle as a static, constant item.

Musk's effect on the allure of electric vehicles stretches out past feel and execution. The organization's Supercharger organization, an organization of quick charging stations, tended to a basic worry for potential EV purchasers — the feeling of dread toward running out of charge during long excursions. By putting resources into and extending the Supercharger organization, Musk and Tesla eased range uneasiness, making electric vehicles more functional and alluring for a more extensive crowd.

One more aspect of Musk's effect on attractiveness is his dominance of promoting and brand picture. Musk's utilization of online entertainment, especially Twitter, has become incredible. His capacity to draw in with the general population, share refreshes, and answer both analysis and commendation progressively has developed a special and strong brand persona. Musk's own image is indivisible from Tesla's, and this has contributed altogether to the allure of Tesla vehicles. The faction like following that Musk has amassed mirrors the profound association that individuals have with both the man and the brand.

Moreover, Musk's nervy ventures and aggressive objectives have caught the public's creative mind and added to the attractiveness of Tesla items. The disclosing of the Tesla Cybertruck, with its flighty plan and commitments of unequaled sturdiness, is a demonstration of Musk's eagerness to oppose show and challenge laid out standards. In any event, when confronted with difficulties, for example, the scandalous "broken glass" occurrence during the Cybertruck uncover, Musk's capacity to transform difficulties into amazing open doors features his effect on molding public discernment and attractiveness.

Musk's effect on execution and allure stretches out past the car area. His work at SpaceX, pushing the limits of room investigation and business space travel, has additionally added to his awesome persona. The fruitful send off and arriving of reusable rockets, the improvement of the Starship space apparatus, and the vision to make humankind a multi-planetary animal categories all add to Musk's story of stretching the boundaries of what is conceivable.

While Musk's effect on execution and allure has without a doubt moved Tesla to the front line of the auto business, it isn't without its debates. Musk's administration style, described by an occasionally reckless and offbeat methodology, has confronted analysis.

From public disagreements via web-based entertainment to fights in court with administrative specialists, Musk's conduct has been a two sided deal, at the same time powering the persona of the Tesla brand and raising worries about corporate administration.

Besides, the imperious dynamic style that Musk encapsulates has been a wellspring of both profound respect and concern. The speed at which choices are made under Musk's administration is exceptional, empowering Tesla to turn rapidly and remain in front of the opposition. Nonetheless, this approach has additionally prompted difficulties, including creation delays, quality control issues, and worries about work environment conditions.

The more extensive effect of Musk's vision goes past the progress of Tesla as an organization. His support for environmentally friendly power, reasonable transportation, and the colonization of Mars has propelled another age of business people and trailblazers. The Musk impact can be seen in the multiplication of electric vehicle new businesses, expanded interest in sustainable power advances, and a recharged center around aggressive objectives in different enterprises.

All in all, Elon Musk's impact on reclassifying execution and allure in the auto business is a complex peculiarity. Through Tesla, Musk has pushed electric vehicles into the standard as well as set new principles for execution, style, and client experience. The effect of Musk's vision reaches out past the car area, impacting public discernment, motivating development, and testing laid out standards chasing a feasible and invigorating future. In any case, likewise with any groundbreaking figure, Musk's heritage is set apart by both worship and analysis, mirroring the intricacies of administration in the always developing scene of innovation and transportation.

Chapter 3

Beyond Cars: Tesla's Holistic Approach

Tesla, under the visionary initiative of Elon Musk, has risen above the ordinary limits of the auto business, embracing a comprehensive methodology that stretches out past vehicles. While the organization is broadly perceived for its noteworthy electric vehicles (EVs), Tesla's impact saturates different areas, including energy, innovation, and foundation. This all encompassing vision not just reclassifies the job of an auto organization yet additionally highlights Musk's obligation to tending to worldwide difficulties through advancement and feasible practices.

At the center of Tesla's all encompassing methodology is the reconciliation of clean energy arrangements into its item biological system. Past assembling electric vehicles, Tesla has wandered into environmentally friendly power items, like sunlight based chargers and energy stockpiling arrangements. The obtaining of SolarCity in 2016 denoted a huge step towards solidifying Tesla's situation as a coordinated economical energy organization. Musk's vision was to make a consistent biological system where electric vehicles, sunlight based energy age, and energy stockpiling work pair to give a complete and feasible arrangement.

Tesla's introduction to sun powered energy is epitomized by the Tesla Sun based Rooftop, an exceptional and stylishly satisfying arrangement that incorporates sun oriented cells into roofing materials. This development permits homes to outfit sun based energy without the requirement for conventional sun powered chargers, mixing supportability with structural plan. The Sunlight based Rooftop epitomizes Musk's obligation to making clean energy open and engaging, testing the idea that sustainable power arrangements must be utilitarian and tastefully unappealing.

Supplementing the Sunlight based Rooftop is Tesla's Powerwall, a home battery stockpiling framework intended to store overabundance energy created by sun powered chargers. The Powerwall not just gives mortgage holders a solid wellspring of reinforcement power yet additionally adds to the general strength and effectiveness of the energy network. By integrating energy stockpiling arrangements into private settings, Musk intends to decentralize and democratize energy creation, diminishing reliance on concentrated power networks and petroleum products.

Tesla's effect on the energy area reaches out past individual homes to the size of whole networks. The Tesla Powerpack and Megapack, huge scope energy capacity arrangements, empower the capacity of environmentally friendly power produced by sources like breeze and sunlight based ranches. These network scale energy capacity arrangements assume a urgent part in settling energy lattices, improving dependability, and working with the combination of irregular environmentally friendly power sources into the more extensive energy foundation.

Notwithstanding energy age and capacity, Tesla's impact on manageability is further clear in its electric vehicle charging framework. The Supercharger organization, started by Tesla, addresses a deliberate work to address the reach uneasiness related with electric vehicles. By decisively setting high velocity charging stations along parkways and in metropolitan places, Tesla has made a thorough organization that permits electric vehicle proprietors to travel significant distances easily.

The Supercharger network represents Musk's ground breaking way to deal with framework improvement. While different automakers at first depended on existing charging foundation or anticipated that outsider elements should fill the hole, Tesla stepped up to the plate and assemble its organization. This proactive methodology not just addressed a basic hindrance to electric vehicle reception yet in addition exhibited Tesla's obligation to giving start to finish answers for its clients, stretching out past the assembling of vehicles.

Past individual purchasers, Tesla has designated the business area with the presentation of the Tesla Semi, an all-electric class 8 truck. Musk's vision for the Tesla Semi stretches out past electric impetus; it includes independent driving capacities, streamlined plan, and upgraded wellbeing highlights. By jolting cargo transport, Tesla plans to diminish emanations in the planned operations industry, testing the customary dependence on diesel-fueled trucks and displaying the adaptability of electric vehicle innovation.

The Tesla Semi likewise coordinates the idea of the "Megacharger," a fast charging arrangement explicitly intended for electric trucks. This foundation improvement is characteristic of Tesla's all encompassing way to deal with charging transportation across different areas. Musk's accentuation on tending to the natural effect of cargo transport lines up with a more extensive obligation to manageability and highlights Tesla's impact on reshaping enterprises past traveler vehicles.

In the domain of computerized reasoning (artificial intelligence) and independent driving, Tesla has arisen as a pioneer. Musk's vision for Tesla vehicles goes past simple transportation; he imagines a future where vehicles can work independently, determined by complex simulated intelligence calculations. The presentation of Autopilot, Tesla's semi-independent driving component, denoted a critical stage towards accomplishing this vision. While full independence stays a work underway and dependent upon administrative endorsement, Musk's obligation to propelling simulated intelligence in vehicles has separate Tesla in the car scene.

The way to deal with artificial intelligence at Tesla includes utilizing genuine information from the whole armada of Tesla vehicles to prepare and further develop the brain networks liable for independent driving. This aggregate educational experience, known as "armada learning," empowers Tesla vehicles to profit from the encounters and bits of knowledge acquired by the whole organization. Musk's methodology of using the immense measures of information created by Tesla vehicles for ceaseless improvement embodies an information driven way to deal with development, where certifiable use turns into an important asset for refining innovation.

The organization of the Full Self-Driving (FSD) highlight, yet in a beta stage, further epitomizes Musk's striking and aggressive way to deal with independent driving. The FSD highlight intends to empower Tesla vehicles to explore complex metropolitan conditions, handle convergences, and answer different traffic situations without human intercession. Musk's steady trust in the capability of independent driving innovation, combined with the iterative sending of elements through programming refreshes, grandstands a pledge to pushing the limits of what is viewed as feasible in the car business.

Musk's impact on innovation and advancement isn't bound to the car area. His endeavors into brain innovation through Neuralink address a bold undertaking to combine the human cerebrum with man-made reasoning. Neuralink, established in 2016, means to foster mind machine interface (BMI) advancements that permit direct correspondence between the human cerebrum and outer gadgets. Musk's vision for Neuralink incorporates tending to neurological problems, upgrading mental capacities, and at last accomplishing beneficial interaction among people and man-made intelligence.

The investigation of mind machine interfaces brings up moral and cultural issues about protection, assent, and the expected ramifications of combining human discernment with outer advances. Musk's association in Neuralink features his obligation to handling complex difficulties at the convergence of innovation and humankind. While the acknowledgment of Neuralink's vision is a drawn out prospect, Musk's readiness to put assets and scholarly capital in such aggressive undertakings highlights his devotion to pushing the limits of what innovation can accomplish.

Tesla's effect on the innovation and assembling areas is likewise obvious in its way to deal with creation processes. The Gigafactories, rambling assembling offices laid out by Tesla, encapsulate Musk's obligation to downsizing creation and driving expenses. The Gigafactory in Nevada, known as Gigafactory 1, addresses a change in perspective in the assembling of lithium-particle batteries. By in an upward direction coordinating battery creation, Tesla planned to accomplish economies of scale and decrease the expense of electric vehicle batteries, a basic part in making electric vehicles more reasonable.

The Gigafactories reach out past the creation of batteries to include vehicle gathering. The Gigafactory in Shanghai, known as Gigafactory 3, addresses Tesla's introduction to the Chinese market and fills in as a model for limited creation. This essential methodology tends to provincial interest all the more productively as well as mitigates the effect of duties and exchange vulnerabilities. Musk's accentuation on laying out Gigafactories overall mirrors a pledge to worldwide extension and versatility.

Tesla's effect on the financial exchange is imperative, described by huge instability and regular changes. The organization's valuation, frequently dependent upon both richness and distrust, reflects financial backer feeling in regards to Musk's aggressive plans and the potential for Tesla to reform different businesses. The stock's versatility, regardless of occasional difficulties and debates, highlights Musk's capacity to motivate certainty among financial backers and position Tesla as a groundbreaking power on the lookout.

Notwithstanding, Musk's authority style and correspondence approach, while adding to Tesla's persona and public commitment, have likewise ignited discussions and legitimate difficulties. Musk's utilization of online entertainment, especially Twitter, to impart organization updates, plans, and individual perspectives has prompted administrative investigation and lawful activities. The exchange between Musk's public persona, Tesla's stock presentation, and the more extensive market elements epitomizes the one of a kind difficulties and potential open doors related with Tesla's comprehensive methodology.

Looking forward, Musk's impact on Tesla's comprehensive methodology is ready to keep forming the direction of the enterprises the organization has entered. The continuous advancement of the Cybertruck, Tesla's entrance into the pickup truck market, the extension of the Supercharger organization, and the ceaseless improvement of simulated intelligence and independent driving abilities embody Musk's constant quest for development and market disturbance. The drawn out effect of Tesla's comprehensive methodology on energy, transportation, and innovation will unfurl after some time, impacting enterprises as well as cultural discernments and assumptions.

All in all, Tesla's comprehensive methodology under the administration of Elon Musk rises above the customary limits of the car business. The coordination of clean energy arrangements, the improvement of independent driving innovation, the introduction to brain innovation, and the accentuation on supportable practices on the whole exhibit Musk's obligation to tending to worldwide difficulties through development. Tesla's effect stretches out past vehicles, impacting energy framework, innovation, assembling, and, surprisingly, the financial exchange. Musk's brassy vision and all encompassing technique highlight the groundbreaking capability of an organization that tries to rethink businesses and add to an additional reasonable and mechanically progressed future.

3.1 . Diversification into Renewable Energy

Broadening into sustainable power addresses an essential shift for organizations and economies looking to moderate ecological effect, decrease reliance on petroleum derivatives, and embrace reasonable practices. Lately, there has been a prominent pattern among organizations, both enormous and little, to differentiate their tasks into environmentally friendly power sources. This shift is driven by a mix of natural cognizance, administrative motivations, and the acknowledgment of the monetary advantages related with environmentally friendly power. Looking at the elements adding to this expansion, the central participants included, and the effect on different ventures gives important bits of knowledge into the more extensive progress towards a maintainable energy future.

The basic for broadening into environmentally friendly power emerges from developing worries about environmental change, air contamination, and the limited idea of petroleum derivative assets. The consuming of petroleum products for energy is a significant supporter of ozone depleting substance outflows, which thus prompts an Earth-wide temperature boost and environment related difficulties. The need to decrease fossil fuel byproducts and change to cleaner energy sources has turned into a worldwide need, inciting organizations to investigate sustainable choices, for example, sunlight based, wind, hydro, and geothermal energy.

One of the essential drivers of broadening into sustainable power is the rising consciousness of the ecological effect of customary energy sources. The extraction, handling, and consuming of non-renewable energy sources discharge poisons up high, water, and soil, adding to air contamination, water tainting, and living space annihilation. As open consciousness of these natural outcomes develops, customers, financial backers, and administrative bodies are forcing organizations to embrace more economical works on, including the consolidation of sustainable power into their activities.

Administrative motivating forces and commands assume a vital part in empowering broadening into sustainable power. Legislatures overall are carrying out approaches that advance the utilization of environmentally friendly power and set focuses for diminishing fossil fuel byproducts.

Impetuses, for example, tax reductions, endowments, and great administrative structures establish an ideal climate for organizations to put resources into sustainable power projects. By adjusting their techniques to these administrative motivators, organizations can add to maintainability objectives as well as advantage from cost investment funds and positive advertising.

Innovative progressions and diminishing expenses related with sustainable power advances have likewise energized expansion. The declining cost of sunlight based chargers, wind turbines, and energy stockpiling frameworks has made sustainable power all the more monetarily feasible for organizations. As the effectiveness of sustainable advancements improves, organizations wind up in a situation to lessen their ecological impression as well as upgrade their drawn out cost seriousness. The combination of innovative advancement and diminishing expenses has made a convincing business case for enhancement into sustainable power.

The expansion into environmentally friendly power isn't restricted to a particular area; rather, it traverses a different scope of businesses. Organizations in the innovation, assembling, retail, and energy areas are progressively integrating environmentally friendly power into their activities. Tech goliaths like Google and Apple have focused on fueling their tasks with 100 percent environmentally friendly power, displaying a position of authority in driving the change towards a feasible energy future. Fabricating organizations, as well, are coordinating sustainable power to control their offices, lessen functional expenses, and line up with corporate maintainability objectives.

In the retail area, key part are utilizing environmentally friendly power to decrease their natural effect as well as meet purchaser assumptions for maintainable practices. Retailers perceive that buyers are turning out to be all the more ecologically cognizant and are settling on buying choices in light of an organization's obligation to maintainability. Thus, expansion into environmentally friendly power turns into an essential move to line up with buyer values and improve brand notoriety.

The energy area itself is going through a change, with customary utilities differentiating their energy portfolios to incorporate more inexhaustible sources. This shift is driven by both administrative prerequisites and market elements. Environmentally friendly power projects, for example, sun oriented and wind ranches, are turning out to be progressively cutthroat with conventional petroleum product based power age. Service organizations are perceiving the monetary advantages of broadening into renewables, including the potential for long haul cost reserve funds and more prominent flexibility despite administrative changes.

The expansion into environmentally friendly power is additionally obvious in the transportation business, where electric vehicles (EVs) controlled by environmentally friendly power sources are building up momentum.

Car makers are putting vigorously in electric and mixture vehicle advancements, lining up with the worldwide shift towards cleaner transportation. The combination of environmentally friendly power into the transportation area isn't restricted to traveler vehicles; it reaches out to transports, trucks, and, surprisingly, oceanic vehicle, further adding to the decrease of ozone harming substance emanations.

The flying business, generally dependent on petroleum derivatives, is likewise investigating ways of differentiating into environmentally friendly power. Manageable flying energizes (SAFs) got from sustainable sources, for example, biofuels, are being tried and carried out as an option in contrast to customary fly powers. While the far and wide reception of sustainable flight energizes is still in the beginning phases, the obligation to finding manageable choices mirrors a more extensive industry affirmation of the need to address the natural effect of air travel.

Environmentally friendly power projects, especially sun based and wind ranches, are turning out to be progressively appealing speculation open doors. Institutional financial backers, including benefits assets and confidential value firms, are enhancing their portfolios by designating assets to environmentally friendly power framework. The solidness and long haul returns related with sustainable power projects make them an engaging choice for financial backers looking for both monetary and natural returns. This flood of venture capital adds to the development and extension of environmentally friendly power framework internationally.

The effect of enhancement into sustainable power stretches out past natural and monetary contemplations; it likewise has social ramifications. The shift towards environmentally friendly power sets out work open doors in the perfect energy area, going from assembling and establishment to upkeep and innovative work. As the environmentally friendly power industry extends, it adds to the production of a talented labor force devoted to reasonable practices. Also, the organization of environmentally friendly power projects in nearby networks can prompt expanded energy freedom and flexibility.

The coordination of environmentally friendly power into corporate procedures includes a blend of on location age, power buy arrangements (PPAs), and interests in environmentally friendly power credits (RECs). On location age, for example, sunlight based chargers on organization premises, permits organizations to deliver clean energy for their activities straightforwardly. PPAs include long haul concurrences with sustainable power project designers, where organizations focus on buying a fore-ordained measure of energy at a decent cost. RECs, then again, address the ecological characteristics of environmentally friendly power age and can be bought to balance an organization's carbon impression.

Corporate responsibilities to 100 percent environmentally friendly power are turning out to be more typical. Organizations that accomplish this achievement are much of the time part of drives, for example, the RE100, a worldwide cooperative exertion that unites organizations focused on obtaining 100 percent sustainable power.

The RE100 drive fills in as a stage for organizations to share best practices, exhibit accomplishments, and motivate others to speed up their progress to sustainable power.

One striking illustration of broadening into environmentally friendly power is Google's accomplishment of being carbon-impartial beginning around 2007 and resolving to work on 100 percent sustainable power by 2020. Google's methodology includes a mix of on location sun based and wind projects, long haul power buy arrangements, and interests in environmentally friendly power foundation. The organization's responsibility stretches out past its immediate tasks to incorporate its whole store network, building up the possibility that expansion into sustainable power requires an exhaustive and cooperative methodology.

Walmart, a key part in the retail area, is one more model of broadening into environmentally friendly power. Walmart put forth an objective to be controlled by 100 percent environmentally friendly power by 2035 and focused on accomplishing no outflows across its worldwide tasks by 2040. The organization is putting resources into on location sunlight based establishments, wind energy undertakings, and energy proficiency estimates across its stores and circulation focuses. Walmart's procedure lines up with its maintainability targets, cost decrease objectives, and responsiveness to client inclinations for naturally cognizant items and practices.

In the car area, Tesla stands apart as a trailblazer in the coordination of environmentally friendly power into its plan of action. Past assembling electric vehicles, Tesla has put resources into energy capacity arrangements and sun powered items. The organization's Gigafactories, where electric vehicle batteries are created, are intended to be fueled by environmentally friendly power. Tesla's Energy division centers around private and business sun based establishments, energy capacity items like the Powerwall and Powerpack, and the advancement of utility-scale energy capacity projects.

Past individual organizations, whole nations are taking critical steps in expanding into environmentally friendly power. Denmark, for instance, has been a pioneer in wind energy, with wind power representing a significant piece of the country's power age. Denmark's obligation to sustainable power reaches out to aggressive targets, including becoming carbon-nonpartisan by 2050. The progress of Denmark in outfitting wind power for both homegrown use and product highlights the monetary and natural advantages of expansion into renewables at a public level.

China, the world's biggest producer of ozone depleting substances, has likewise set out on an excursion of broadening into sustainable power. The nation leads all around the world in the creation and arrangement of sun powered chargers and electric vehicles. China's interests in wind and sunlight based power, combined with its obligation to top fossil fuel byproducts by 2030 and accomplish carbon nonpartisanship by 2060, mirror a far reaching methodology to change towards a more feasible and low-carbon energy framework.

While the advantages of expansion into environmentally friendly power are clear, difficulties and contemplations should be explored to guarantee an effective change. The discontinuous idea of environmentally friendly power sources, for example, sunlight based and wind, presents difficulties to framework solidness and unwavering quality. High level energy stockpiling advances, framework modernization, and inventive arrangements are fundamental for address the fluctuation of sustainable power and guarantee a dependable power supply.

The underlying capital expenses related with sustainable power ventures can be a boundary for certain organizations, particularly little and medium-sized endeavors (SMEs). Notwithstanding, as innovation advances and economies of scale are understood, the expenses of sustainable power establishments are supposed to keep diminishing, making them more open to a more extensive scope of organizations.

Administrative and strategy systems assume a urgent part in working with or preventing the broadening into sustainable power. Clear and predictable guidelines, alongside steady strategies and motivators, establish a helpful climate for organizations to put resources into sustainable power projects. On the other hand, dubious or negative administrative circumstances can stop venture and slow the reception of environmentally friendly power.

The coordination of environmentally friendly power into existing frameworks requires cautious preparation and thought of specialized, calculated, and monetary variables. Organizations should survey their energy needs, assess the achievability of on location age or power buy arrangements, and adjust their environmentally friendly power methodology to more extensive supportability objectives. Cooperative endeavors between organizations, states, and networks are fundamental to understanding the maximum capacity of enhancement into environmentally friendly power.

The enhancement into sustainable power is definitely not a one-size-fits-all arrangement; rather, it includes a nuanced and setting explicit methodology. Various businesses, areas, and organizations will confront novel difficulties and open doors in view of their functional setting, energy prerequisites, and administrative conditions. By and by, the overall pattern towards embracing environmentally friendly power means an extraordinary change in how organizations and economies see and use energy assets.

All in all, the broadening into sustainable power addresses a change in perspective driven by natural goals, administrative motivations, and financial contemplations. Organizations across different areas are perceiving the need to progress towards practical energy sources, not exclusively to diminish their natural effect yet additionally to stay serious in a quickly developing business sector.

The joining of environmentally friendly power into corporate procedures, whether through on location age, power buy arrangements, or interests in sustainable power projects, mirrors a promise to long haul manageability and versatility. As the world keeps on wrestling with the difficulties of environmental change, the energy behind broadening into sustainable power is probably going to speed up, making ready for a more manageable and versatile energy future.

3.2 . The Role of Solar Technology in Musk's Vision

Elon Musk's vision stretches out a long ways past the domain of electric vehicles and space investigation; it includes a key change of energy frameworks. Fundamental to Musk's vision is the critical job of sun powered innovation in reshaping the manner in which the world creates and consumes energy. Through drives, for example, Tesla's sun based items and the procurement of SolarCity, Musk intends to speed up the change to feasible energy by saddling the force of the sun. This vision mirrors a comprehensive way to deal with tending to environmental change, decreasing reliance on petroleum products, and making a more economical future.

At the center of Musk's sun powered vision is the acknowledgment of the sun as a bountiful and sustainable wellspring of energy. Sun based innovation, especially sun oriented photovoltaic (PV) boards, permits the change of daylight into power. Musk imagines a future where sun based power turns into a pervasive and prevailing wellspring of energy, giving spotless and reasonable power to homes, organizations, and, surprisingly, whole urban communities.

Tesla's introduction to sun powered innovation is exemplified by the Sun oriented Rooftop, a historic item that consistently incorporates sun based cells into roofing materials. Not at all like customary sunlight based chargers that are mounted on top of existing rooftops, the Sun powered Rooftop replaces regular roofing materials with sun oriented tiles. This imaginative methodology catches sun powered energy proficiently as well as upgrades the style of structures, tending to a typical worry about the visual effect of sun based establishments.

The Sun powered Rooftop's plan, roused by different material styles, consolidates usefulness with tastefulness. Musk's accentuation on feel mirrors a comprehension that the far reaching reception of sunlight based innovation requires arrangements that mix consistently with existing foundation and take special care of different engineering inclinations. By making sun oriented innovation outwardly engaging and flexible, Musk tries to defeat hindrances to reception and empower the mix of sun based power into the fabricated climate.

Notwithstanding the Sunlight based Rooftop, Tesla offers sun powered chargers and sun oriented energy capacity arrangements through its Powerwall and Powerpack items. These energy stockpiling frameworks, combined with sun powered chargers, empower clients to store overabundance energy created during the day for use during times of low daylight or high energy interest.

The joining of sun powered chargers with energy capacity tends to one of the vital difficulties of sun oriented power — the irregular idea of daylight — and improves the dependability and proficiency of sun based energy frameworks.

Musk's sun powered vision reaches out past individual families to incorporate whole networks and even nations. The idea of a "sunlight based fueled future" includes enormous scope sun powered establishments, for example, sun oriented ranches and sunlight based parks, that can produce huge measures of power. Musk imagines a decentralized energy framework where neighborhood networks produce, store, and deal with their energy through a mix of sunlight based innovation, energy capacity, and savvy matrix arrangements. This vision lines up with the more extensive pattern of moving towards a stronger, dispersed, and reasonable energy framework.

The procurement of SolarCity in 2016 assumed a huge part in solidifying Tesla's situation as a thorough energy arrangements supplier. SolarCity, helped to establish by Musk's cousins Lyndon and Peter Rive, was a main sun powered energy administrations organization that zeroed in on sun oriented establishments for private, business, and modern clients. By coordinating SolarCity into Tesla, Musk meant to smooth out the collaboration between electric vehicles, energy capacity, and sun powered innovation, making an incorporated biological system that tends to different features of the energy challenge.

The SolarCity obtaining likewise situated Tesla as a player in the sun based renting and supporting business sector. Musk's methodology included making sunlight based establishments more available to a more extensive crowd by offering funding choices and rent arrangements. This approach expected to conquer the forthright expense obstruction related with sunlight based innovation, making it monetarily practical for mortgage holders and organizations to embrace sun oriented power without critical capital speculation.

Musk's sun oriented vision is unpredictably associated with the more extensive setting of environmental change and the earnest need to progress away from petroleum products. The consuming of non-renewable energy sources for power age is a significant supporter of ozone depleting substance discharges, driving environmental change and its related effects. Musk considers sun oriented innovation to be a critical answer for decarbonizing the energy area, lessening dependence on limited petroleum product assets, and moderating the natural effect of power age.

The worldwide shift towards sustainable power lines up with Musk's sun based vision, and he effectively advances speeding up this change. Musk perceives the significance of cooperation and aggregate activity in tending to environmental change, and he frequently advocates for a quicker progress to practical energy arrangements.

Through drives like the Gigafactory, where both electric vehicle batteries and sun based items are fabricated, Musk expects to downsize up creation and drive costs, making sun powered innovation more open and reasonable on a worldwide scale.

Notwithstanding private and business applications, Musk imagines the job of sun oriented innovation in controlling transportation. The combination of sunlight based chargers into electric vehicles, especially through the execution of sun powered rooftops on vehicles, is a thought Musk has investigated. While the flow effectiveness of sunlight based chargers on vehicles might be restricted because of the size requirements of vehicles, Musk sees expected in progressing sun oriented innovation to improve the reach and productivity of electric vehicles. This vision lines up with Musk's general objective of making an economical and energy-free future.

The effect of Musk's sun powered vision stretches out to creating locales and regions with restricted admittance to conventional power framework. Musk perceives that the decentralized and measured nature of sunlight based innovation makes it appropriate for giving off-matrix power arrangements. Through projects like the Tesla Sunlight based Microgrid in Kauai, Hawaii, Musk has shown the capability of sun oriented innovation to drive whole networks freely of conventional framework foundation. This approach holds guarantee for tending to energy destitution and advancing feasible improvement in locales where admittance to power is a test.

Musk's sun oriented vision isn't without difficulties and contemplations. The productivity and cost-adequacy of sun powered innovation, while improving, still require continuous advancement and venture. Propels in energy capacity innovations, matrix combination, and the improvement of savvy framework are fundamental parts of understanding Musk's vision for a sun oriented controlled future. Furthermore, administrative systems and strategies that help the far and wide reception of sun powered innovation assume a critical part in molding the direction of the sun oriented energy industry.

The monetary feasibility of sunlight based innovation is a critical figure driving its reception. Musk's accentuation on economies of scale, as obvious in the Gigafactory model, mirrors an essential way to deal with lessening the expense of sun oriented items. By expanding creation volumes and streamlining fabricating processes, Musk expects to make sun oriented innovation more serious with customary energy sources. The outcome of this procedure is clear in the diminishing expense of sunlight powered chargers over the course of the last 10 years, making sun oriented energy progressively open to a more extensive crowd.

Musk's sunlight based vision crosses with other groundbreaking advances and ideas he is effectively seeking after. The improvement of energy stockpiling arrangements, for example, the Powerwall and Powerpack, supplements the irregular idea of sun oriented power, empowering a more solid and persistent energy supply.

The combination of sun based innovation with electric vehicles and independent driving addresses a synergistic methodology towards making a thorough and reasonable transportation environment.

The cultural effect of Musk's sun oriented vision reaches out to work creation, advancement, and the strengthening of people and networks. The development of the sunlight based industry adds to the making of talented positions in assembling, establishment, support, and innovative work. The democratization of energy through decentralized sun oriented establishments enables people to become energy makers, decreasing reliance on unified utilities and cultivating a feeling of energy freedom.

Musk's support for a sunlight based controlled future isn't restricted to Tesla; it stretches out to his contribution in different endeavors. SolarCity, SpaceX's dependence on sunlight based power for space missions, and Musk's commitment to the sustainable power area through associations like the OpenAI exhibit a reliable obligation to progressing reasonable and ground breaking arrangements. Musk's impact arrives at past his organizations; he fills in as an impetus for far reaching change and joint effort towards a common objective of a more maintainable future.

All in all, Elon Musk's sun oriented vision addresses a visionary and groundbreaking way to deal with reshaping the worldwide energy scene. Through Tesla's sun oriented items, the procurement of SolarCity, and an extensive biological system that coordinates sun based innovation with electric vehicles and energy stockpiling, Musk looks to speed up the change to practical energy. His vision reaches out past individual items to include a comprehensive and decentralized energy foundation fueled by the sun. While challenges exist, Musk's obligation to development, economies of scale, and a practical future positions sun powered innovation as a focal support point in his more extensive mission to address environmental change and make a stronger and naturally cognizant world.

Tesla, a spearheading force in the car business, has arisen not just as a vehicle maker but rather as a defender of a comprehensive methodology towards transportation. Past the regular extent of cars, Tesla imagines a future where manageable energy, state of the art innovation, and natural cognizance unite to reclassify the whole transportation biological system. This synopsis dives into the complex components of Tesla's all encompassing methodology, investigating the organization's introduction to electric vehicles, environmentally friendly power, and interconnected frameworks that reach out past the limits of customary auto limits.

At the center of Tesla's groundbreaking vision is the obligation to electric vehicles (EVs) as a way to change individual and public transportation. Tesla's electric vehicles, like the Model S, Model 3, Model X, and Model Y, have set new benchmarks for execution as well as assumed an essential part in dispersing the fantasy that electric vehicles think twice about power and reach.

With progressions in battery innovation, Tesla has expanded the scope of its EVs, mitigating the longstanding worry of "range nervousness" and making electric vehicles a practical choice for a more extensive crowd.

Besides, Tesla's commitment to manageable energy is encapsulated by its Gigafactories, rambling offices decisively situated all over the planet to make batteries and sustainable power items at a remarkable scale. These Gigafactories not just add to the large scale manufacturing of electric vehicles yet in addition underline Tesla's more extensive obligation to speeding up the world's progress to supportable energy. The organization's interest in environmentally friendly power sources, for example, sun based and wind power, lines up with its objective of making a coordinated energy biological system that limits reliance on non-sustainable assets.

Independent driving innovation remains as one more mainstay of Tesla's all encompassing methodology. The arrangement of cutting edge driver-help frameworks (ADAS) and Full Self-Driving (FSD) capacities highlights Tesla's desire to rethink the connection among people and their vehicles. While the innovation is consistently advancing, Tesla's Autopilot highlight has previously exhibited critical steps towards accomplishing independent driving, with customary over-the-air refreshes upgrading the framework's capacities and extending its usefulness.

Tesla's effect stretches out past individual vehicles, as the organization imagines an organization of interconnected frameworks that by and large reclassify the transportation scene. The Tesla Supercharger network embodies this vision, giving a quick charging foundation that upholds really long travel for Tesla vehicles. This essential framework speculation not just addresses one of the essential worries related with electric vehicles — charging time — yet in addition encourages a feeling of local area among Tesla proprietors, building up the brand's character and obligation to practical transportation.

Notwithstanding its undertakings in electric vehicles and supportable energy, Tesla has wandered into the domain of energy stockpiling arrangements. The Powerwall and Powerpack are imaginative items intended to store overabundance energy created from sustainable sources, taking into consideration a more predictable and dependable power supply. These energy stockpiling arrangements contribute not exclusively to the maintainability of individual families yet additionally to the steadiness of the more extensive electrical network.

Past the substantial items, Tesla's introduction to programming improvement is a demonstration of its comprehensive methodology. Customary programming refreshes, conveyed over-the-air, upgrade the presentation, security, and usefulness of Tesla vehicles. This approach separates Tesla from conventional automakers as well as mirrors a promise to nonstop improvement and transformation to developing mechanical scenes.

In addition, Tesla's entrance into the energy market through its procurement of SolarCity epitomizes its comprehensive vision. By coordinating sun based energy age, energy capacity, and electric vehicles, Tesla tries to make a consistent and manageable energy environment. The collaboration between these parts not just upgrades the general proficiency of the framework yet additionally adds to lessening the carbon impression related with conventional energy sources.

Tesla's effect on the car business goes past its job as a disruptor; it typifies a change in perspective in how society sees and connects with transportation. The organization's obligation to maintainability, mechanical development, and interconnected frameworks positions it as a pioneer in the continuous development of transportation. While difficulties and cynics endure, Tesla's constant quest for its all encompassing vision keeps on molding the eventual fate of versatility.

As Tesla keeps on pushing the limits of advancement, its impact reaches out to enterprises past auto. The organization's progressions in battery innovation, electric drive, and sustainable power have extensive ramifications for areas like aviation, sea, and public transportation. The gradually expanding influence of Tesla's advancements isn't bound to the domain of individual vehicles however stretches out to different aspects of worldwide versatility.

In the domain of room investigation, Tesla's pioneer, Elon Musk, simultaneously drives SpaceX, a confidential aviation producer and space transportation organization. The exchange between Musk's endeavors in electric vehicles and space investigation highlights a more extensive vision of humankind's future. Tesla's advancements in battery innovation, significant for the productivity of electric vehicles, likewise track down application in controlling satellites and space apparatus, adding to the manageability of room investigation.

Besides, Tesla's impact is unmistakable in the sea business, where zap is building up forward momentum as a way to diminish outflows and improve maintainability. The very battery innovation that controls Tesla's electric vehicles tracks down applications in electric impetus frameworks for ships. The improvement of electric boats and ships grandstands the versatility of Tesla's mechanical headways, offering a brief look into a future where even the oceans are explored with a guarantee to ecological protection.

Public transportation remains as another field where Tesla's all encompassing methodology reverberates. While the organization fundamentally centers around individual electric vehicles, the standards of feasible energy and interconnected frameworks can possibly reshape public travel. The joining of electric transports, fueled by Tesla's innovation, combined with an exhaustive charging foundation, could upset metropolitan versatility and fundamentally diminish the ecological effect of mass travel frameworks.

Tesla's effect on the car and transportation areas additionally stretches out to the more extensive economy. The organization's accentuation on homegrown assembling, as confirmed by its Gigafactories in different nations, adds to work creation and monetary development. The interest for unrefined components, like lithium and cobalt for batteries, has prodded investigation and mining exercises, further animating financial action in related businesses.

Be that as it may, Tesla's comprehensive methodology isn't without its difficulties and discussions. Concerns with respect to the natural effect of battery creation, moral mining rehearses, and the removal of electric vehicle batteries suggest complex conversation starters that request extensive arrangements. Also, the moral ramifications of independent driving innovation, information protection concerns, and administrative obstacles highlight the unpredictable scene in which Tesla works.

The monetary scene encompassing Tesla is similarly powerful. The organization's stock valuation has encountered extraordinary unpredictability, mirroring a blend of financial backer excitement, market hypothesis, and the intrinsic vulnerabilities related with an industry amidst change. The changes in Tesla's stock cost, while demonstrative of the powerful idea of the market, likewise bring up issues about the drawn out manageability of such valuations and the possible effect on the more extensive monetary environment.

As Tesla proceeds to advance and extend its impact, the cultural ramifications of its comprehensive methodology come to the very front. The change to electric vehicles, sustainable power, and interconnected transportation frameworks addresses a mechanical shift as well as a social and conduct change. The acknowledgment and reception of electric vehicles mean a takeoff from the customary dependence on gas powered motors, testing laid out standards and insights encompassing individual transportation.

Taking everything into account, Tesla's comprehensive methodology rises above the traditional limits of the car business, including electric vehicles, environmentally friendly power, interconnected frameworks, and then some. The organization's vision, led by Elon Musk, stretches out to assorted areas, molding the fate of transportation, space investigation, oceanic travel, and public travel. As Tesla explores the intricacies of a quickly developing scene, the cultural, financial, and natural ramifications of its developments highlight the groundbreaking force of a comprehensive way to deal with transportation. Tesla's process isn't just about vehicles; it is an excursion towards rethinking how humankind moves, interfaces, and supports itself in the years to come.

Chapter 4

The Gigafactory Revolution

The Gigafactory upset, led by Elon Musk and Tesla, addresses an extraordinary change in assembling and energy stockpiling. The idea of the Gigafactory arose out of the need to increase creation of electric vehicles (EVs) and energy stockpiling arrangements, like batteries, to fulfill the developing need for practical and clean energy advancements. Musk's vision for Gigafactories reaches out past customary assembling; it is an essential drop to drive down costs, upgrade effectiveness, and reform whole ventures. Analyzing the advancement, effect, and future capability of the Gigafactory model gives bits of knowledge into its job in forming the fate of transportation, energy capacity, and then some.

The expression "Gigafactory" is a portmanteau of "giga," alluding to the billion-watt long periods of battery limit the offices plan to create, and "production line," featuring their enormous scope. The Gigafactory idea began from the acknowledgment that the conventional assembling approach for batteries and electric vehicles was not adequately adaptable to help the mass reception of EVs and far reaching execution of environmentally friendly power stockpiling. Musk imagined a change in outlook in assembling that would reflect the remarkable development found in innovation areas, where economies of scale and large scale manufacturing lead to cost decreases and expanded openness.

The primary Gigafactory, known as Gigafactory 1, was reported by Tesla in 2013 and is situated close to Reno, Nevada. The office was decisively situated to act as a center point for battery creation, explicitly lithium-particle batteries utilized in Tesla's electric vehicles and energy items. Gigafactory 1 was intended to be an in an upward direction coordinated office, consolidating battery cell creation, module gathering, and pack get together under one rooftop. This joining planned to smooth out the creation interaction, decrease store network intricacies, and accomplish cost efficiencies.

The Gigafactory model addresses a takeoff from the conventional act of re-appropriating parts and gathering to different providers. Musk's vision included merging the whole battery fabricating process, from unrefined substances to completed items, inside a solitary office. This approach enhanced calculated processes as well as considered more tight command over quality, creation courses of events, and expenses. The upward mix innate in the Gigafactory model mirrors Musk's obligation to effectiveness, development, and versatility.

Gigafactory, endless supply of its development stages, became one of the biggest assembling offices worldwide, with an impression of over 5.5 million square feet. The size of the office was intended to help the development of batteries for Tesla's electric vehicles, including the Model 3, Model S, and Model X, as well as energy stockpiling items like the Powerwall and Powerpack. The sheer extent of Gigafactory 1 highlighted Musk's aspiration to address not just the auto business' shift towards electric versatility yet additionally the more extensive test of changing to supportable energy frameworks.

One of the vital goals of the Gigafactory model is to accomplish economies of scale in battery creation. The sheer volume of batteries created at Gigafactories is expected to drive down the expense each kilowatt-hour, making electric vehicles more reasonable and energy capacity arrangements more available. Musk's system is established in the conviction that diminishing the expense of batteries is crucial to speeding up the reception of electric vehicles and environmentally friendly power stockpiling on a worldwide scale.

The Gigafactory's effect on the electric vehicle market is critical. The expanded creation limit permits Tesla to fulfill the developing need for its electric vehicles, especially the more reasonable Model 3. As creation volumes increment, the expense of assembling diminishes, empowering Tesla to offer electric vehicles at cutthroat costs contrasted with conventional gas powered motor vehicles. This value equality is a basic calculate persuading customers to do the change to electric vehicles, adding to the more extensive objective of diminishing the carbon impression of the transportation area.

Gigafactory 1 likewise assumed a focal part in the development of Tesla's energy stockpiling items. The Powerwall, a private energy stockpiling arrangement, and the Powerpack, intended for business and modern applications, profited from the expanded creation proficiency and cost decreases accomplished through the Gigafactory model.

By delivering batteries at scale, Tesla meant to make energy capacity arrangements all the more monetarily feasible for a more extensive scope of clients, including mortgage holders, organizations, and service organizations.

The outcome of Gigafactory 1 established the groundwork for resulting Gigafactories and further cycles of the model. Gigafactory Shanghai, situated in China, denoted a critical achievement in Tesla's worldwide extension system. Reported in 2018 and functional since late 2019, Gigafactory Shanghai addresses Tesla's most memorable assembling office outside the US. This essential move was driven by the acknowledgment of China as the biggest electric vehicle market internationally and the need to confine creation to take care of provincial interest.

Gigafactory Shanghai follows the Gigafactory model, zeroing in on the development of electric vehicles for the Chinese market. The office makes the Model 3 and, all the more as of late, the Model Y, Tesla's minimal SUV. By laying out neighborhood creation capacities, Tesla mitigates import levies, diminishes delivering costs, and limits cash trade chances. Moreover, Gigafactory Shanghai fills in as a demonstration of Musk's vision of quickly sending Gigafactories to meet the particular requirements of key business sectors.

The progress of Gigafactory Shanghai is clear in its capacity to rapidly increase creation. The office accomplished volume creation in a surprisingly short time span, exhibiting the versatility and flexibility of the Gigafactory model. Musk's essential way to deal with restriction and market-explicit creation mirrors a profound comprehension of the worldwide elements of the electric vehicle market and the significance of being nimble because of provincial requests and administrative scenes.

The following cycle of the Gigafactory model is Gigafactory Berlin, situated in Grünheide, Germany. Reported in 2019 and under development at the hour of composing, Gigafactory Berlin addresses Tesla's obligation to extending its assembling impression in Europe. The office is supposed to create batteries, battery packs, and powertrains, notwithstanding electric vehicles. Musk's vision for Gigafactory Berlin lines up with the more extensive European push towards electric portability and sustainable power.

Gigafactory Berlin integrates illustrations gained from past Gigafactories and means to set new norms for supportability and natural effect. Musk stressed the utilization of environmentally friendly power, water reusing, and high level assembling cycles to limit the biological impression of the office. The joining of natural contemplations into the plan and activity of Gigafactory Berlin mirrors Musk's obligation to maintainability and lines up with the more extensive industry pattern towards green assembling rehearses.

Gigafactory Texas, situated in Austin, Texas, addresses one more achievement in the Gigafactory development. Declared in 2020, Gigafactory Texas is imagined to be an assembling center point for Tesla's electric vehicles, including the Cybertruck, Tesla's all-electric pickup truck. The choice to lay out Gigafactory Texas highlights Musk's acknowledgment of the essential significance of the U.S. market and the potential for electric vehicles in the pickup truck fragment, generally overwhelmed by ignition motor vehicles.

The Gigafactory model stretches out past Tesla's center business of electric vehicles and energy stockpiling. Musk's vision for Gigafactories incorporates the development of other basic parts for economical energy frameworks. Remarkably, Tesla's emphasis on energy capacity arrangements, for example, the Megapack intended for utility-scale projects, lines up with the more extensive pattern towards framework scale energy capacity. Gigafactories assume a critical part in increasing the creation of these energy stockpiling arrangements, adding to the solidness and flexibility of energy lattices.

The Gigafactory insurgency reaches out past Tesla, impacting the more extensive scene of assembling and energy stockpiling. The progress of the Gigafactory model has incited different organizations to investigate comparable ways to deal with down-size up creation and drive costs. The lithium-particle battery market, specifically, has seen a flood in Gigafactory-like drives from different players looking to satisfy the developing need for batteries in electric vehicles, customer gadgets, and sustainable power projects.

The Gigafactory insurgency isn't restricted to electric vehicles and energy stock-piling; it converges with Musk's more extensive vision for reasonable energy and trans-portation. The combination of Gigafactories with different drives, like Tesla's sunlight based items and headways in computerized reasoning for independent driving, mirrors Musk's comprehensive way to deal with tending to the difficulties of environmental change and encouraging a progress to an economical future.

Musk's vision for Gigafactories lines up with the more extensive industry pattern towards Industry 4.0, described by the mix of advanced innovations, robotization, and information driven decision-production into assembling processes. The Gigafac-tory model integrates progressed advanced mechanics, man-made consciousness, and shrewd assembling standards to improve effectiveness, decrease squander, and stream-line creation work processes. This computerized change of assembling lines up with Musk's general objective of pushing the limits of development and innovation.

The Gigafactory upheaval has not been without difficulties and debates. The sheer scale and quick organization of Gigafactories have raised natural worries and confronted resistance from neighborhood networks.

Issues connected with water utilization, deforestation, and expected influences on biodiversity have been subjects of investigation and administrative difficulties. Musk's reaction to these worries mirrors a continuous obligation to address ecological con-templations and work towards feasible assembling rehearses.

All in all, the Gigafactory upheaval addresses a vital second in the development of assembling and energy stockpiling. Elon Musk's vision for Gigafactories as center points of advancement, effectiveness, and versatility has reshaped the scene of electric vehicles, energy capacity, and feasible energy frameworks. The progress of Gigafactory 1, Gigafactory Shanghai, and the continuous development of Gigafactory Berlin and Gigafactory Texas highlights the extraordinary capability of Musk's vision. The Gigafactory model not just speeds up the progress to manageable transportation and energy yet additionally sets new principles for assembling in the advanced age. As Gigafactories proceed to develop and multiply, their effect on ventures and economies will be a characterizing component of the progress towards an additional feasible and zapped future.

4.1 . Concept and Implementation of Gigafactories

The idea and execution of Gigafactories address a progressive way to deal with assembling, spearheaded by Elon Musk and Tesla. These huge offices, intended for the enormous scope creation of electric vehicles (EVs), batteries, and energy stockpiling arrangements, typify Musk's vision for speeding up the change to practical energy. The expression "Gigafactory" itself mirrors the aggressive size of these offices, each expected to create gigawatt-long stretches of batteries and reshape enterprises. Inspecting the starting points, plan standards, and effect of Gigafactories gives experiences into their job as impetuses for development, cost decrease, and the change of transportation and energy areas.

The beginning of the Gigafactory idea can be followed back to the acknowledgment that the current assembling foundation for electric vehicles and batteries was lacking to fulfill the needs of a quickly developing business sector. In 2013, Elon Musk uncovered the vision for Gigafactory 1, arranged close to Reno, Nevada, to address this bottleneck. The essential goal was clear: proportional up creation, accomplish economies of scale, and fundamentally lessen the expense of batteries, which comprised a significant part of the general expense of EVs.

Integral to the Gigafactory idea is its takeoff from customary assembling models. As opposed to depending on an organization of providers for different parts, Gigafactories embrace an in an upward direction coordinated approach. This implies bringing different phases of the creation cycle under one rooftop, from unrefined substances to completed items. By solidifying the whole store network inside a solitary office, Musk meant to smooth out tasks, wipe out calculated intricacies, and oversee quality and cost.

Gigafactory 1, as the model for ensuing Gigafactories, centers essentially around battery creation. The office incorporates the assembling of battery cells, modules, and packs, guaranteeing a consistent progression of creation from the underlying stages to the eventual outcome. This upward joining takes into consideration more tight coordination between processes, diminishing lead times and limiting the requirement for broad transportation of parts between various offices.

The plan standards of Gigafactories consolidate Musk's tenacious quest for effectiveness and development. The massive size of these offices is deliberate, with Gigafactory 1 covering over 5.5 million square feet upon fulfillment. Gigafactories are not simply enormous assembling plants; they are multi-layered edifices that house innovative work offices, battery creation lines, vehicle gathering segments, and space for future development. This comprehensive methodology lines up with Musk's vision of making self-supporting biological systems equipped for developing with mechanical progressions.

Energy effectiveness is a foundation of the Gigafactory model. Gigafactory 1, for example, uses environmentally friendly power sources, for example, sunlight based and wind power, to a huge degree. The incorporation of sunlight based chargers on the office's rooftop and neighboring ground regions adds to a decreased carbon impression and lines up with Tesla's more extensive obligation to manageability. This accentuation on sustainable power sources highlights Musk's commitment to ecological obligation as well as positions Gigafactories as models for green assembling in a time of expanding natural cognizance.

Past their actual impression and energy framework, Gigafactories typify mechanical development. High level assembling strategies, computerization, and mechanical technology assume a crucial part in accomplishing productivity and accuracy at scale. The joining of Industry 4.0 standards, described by the incorporation of computerized advances into assembling processes, guarantees that Gigafactories are at the bleeding edge of current assembling. Musk's hug of state of the art innovations mirrors a promise to constant improvement and transformation to the developing scene of modern creation.

The effect of Gigafactories is significant, with expansive ramifications for the electric vehicle market, energy capacity industry, and then some. The economies of scale accomplished through Gigafactories contribute fundamentally to the decrease of the expense of batteries, a basic part in EVs and energy stockpiling arrangements. This decrease in cost has a flowing impact, making electric vehicles more reasonable for buyers and energy stockpiling arrangements all the more financially feasible for a scope of uses.

The progress of Gigafactories in driving down costs plays had a significant impact in changing the electric vehicle market. Quite possibly of the main result has been the expanded reasonableness of Tesla's electric vehicles, especially the Model 3.

The Model 3, situated as a mass-market electric vehicle, has become one of the most incredible selling electric vehicles internationally. The effect of Gigafactories in making electric vehicles more available lines up with Musk's more extensive mission of speeding up the world's change to manageable energy.

The Gigafactory model reaches out past electric vehicles to incorporate the creation of batteries and energy stockpiling arrangements. The adaptable creation limit of Gigafactories empowers Tesla to fulfill the developing need for batteries in its electric vehicles as well as for private, business, and utility-scale energy capacity projects. The Powerwall, Powerpack, and Megapack, intended for home use, business applications, and framework scale projects separately, benefit from the productivity and cost-adequacy accomplished through the Gigafactory model.

Gigafactories add to the security and versatility of energy networks by working with the creation of energy stockpiling arrangements. The Megapack, specifically, is intended for enormous scope utility tasks and addresses a stage towards network scale energy capacity. By sending Megapacks, energy suppliers can store overabundance energy produced during times of low interest and delivery it during top interest, improving the effectiveness and unwavering quality of energy frameworks. This utilization of Gigafactories lines up with the more extensive pattern of coordinating sustainable power into existing power frameworks.

The effect of Gigafactories stretches out to work creation, with every office turning into a center point for work in its particular district. The different scope of exercises inside a Gigafactory, from innovative work to assembling and operations, requires a talented and specific labor force. This occupation creation upholds the neighborhood economy as well as adds to the improvement of a labor force with skill in state of the art fabricating advances and practical energy arrangements.

Gigafactories are not bound to the development of electric vehicles and energy stockpiling; they assume an essential part in propelling Musk's more extensive vision for a manageable future. The Gigafactory model crosses with other key drives, like Tesla's sun powered items and progressions in computerized reasoning for independent driving. The incorporation of Gigafactories with these drives mirrors Musk's comprehensive way to deal with tending to the difficulties of environmental change and encouraging a progress to economical transportation and energy frameworks.

The progress of Gigafactory 1 incited Tesla to universally reproduce the model. Gigafactory Shanghai, situated in China, denoted a critical achievement in Tesla's development methodology. The choice to lay out a Gigafactory in China was vital, given China's situation as the biggest electric vehicle market worldwide. Gigafactory Shanghai, functional since late 2019, centers around the creation of the Model 3 and, all the more as of late, the Model Y. This limitation of creation lessens import duties, brings down transportation costs, and lines up with Musk's way of thinking of adjusting to territorial requests.

Gigafactory Berlin, situated in Grünheide, Germany, addresses the following period of Gigafactory extension. Declared in 2019 and under development at the hour of composing, Gigafactory Berlin is supposed to deliver batteries, battery packs, and powertrains, notwithstanding electric vehicles. Musk's vision for Gigafactory Berlin lines up with the more extensive European push towards electric versatility and sustainable power. The office is ready to assume a crucial part in satisfying the need for electric vehicles in the European market.

Gigafactory Texas, arranged in Austin, Texas, reported in 2020, is intended to be an assembling center for Tesla's electric vehicles, including the Cybertruck. The choice to lay out Gigafactory Texas highlights Musk's acknowledgment of the essential significance of the U.S. market and the potential for electric vehicles in the pickup truck fragment. Gigafactory Texas addresses a huge interest in the U.S. car area and adds to the reshaping of the country's auto scene.

The Gigafactory upheaval isn't bound to Tesla; it has impacted the more extensive scene of assembling and energy stockpiling. The progress of the Gigafactory model has incited different organizations to investigate comparable ways to deal with downsize up creation and drive costs. The lithium-particle battery market, specifically, has seen a flood in Gigafactory-like drives from different players trying to satisfy the developing need for batteries in electric vehicles, shopper hardware, and sustainable power projects.

The Gigafactory transformation isn't without difficulties and discussions. The fast sending and monstrous size of Gigafactories have raised ecological worries and confronted resistance from neighborhood networks. Issues connected with water use, deforestation, and likely effects on biodiversity have been subjects of investigation and administrative difficulties. Musk's reaction to these worries mirrors a continuous obligation to address natural contemplations and work towards maintainable assembling rehearses.

All in all, the idea and execution of Gigafactories address a change in outlook in assembling and energy stockpiling. Elon Musk's vision for Gigafactories as impetuses for development, effectiveness, and adaptability has reshaped the scene of electric vehicles, energy capacity, and feasible energy frameworks. The progress of Gigafactory 1, Gigafactory Shanghai, and the continuous development of Gigafactory Berlin and Gigafactory Texas highlights the groundbreaking capability of Musk's vision. The Gigafactory model not just speeds up the progress to economical transportation and energy yet additionally sets new principles for assembling in the advanced age. As Gigafactories proceed to develop and multiply, their effect on ventures and economies will be a characterizing component of the progress towards an additional reasonable and jolted future.

4.2 . Achieving Scale and Efficiency in Battery Production

Accomplishing scale and productivity in battery creation is a basic part of propelling electric vehicles (EVs) and environmentally friendly power stockpiling arrangements. The progress of electric versatility and manageable energy frameworks depends on the capacity to deliver batteries at a huge scope while driving down costs. Elon Musk and Tesla, through their Gigafactories, have been at the very front of reclassifying the scene of battery creation. Looking at the procedures, developments, and difficulties related with accomplishing scale and effectiveness in battery creation gives bits of knowledge into the groundbreaking effect on the electric vehicle market and the more extensive change to economical energy.

One of the major difficulties in the broad reception of electric vehicles has been the expense of batteries. Batteries comprise a significant piece of the general expense of an electric vehicle, making them a deciding variable in the vehicle's reasonableness. Perceiving this test, Elon Musk set off to accomplish economies of scale in battery creation as a way to drive down expenses and make electric vehicles more open to a more extensive market.

The idea of Gigafactories arose as an essential answer for this test. The sheer size of these offices, intended to create gigawatt-long periods of batteries, takes into consideration large scale manufacturing and cost decrease through economies of scale. Gigafactories coordinate the whole battery fabricating process, from unrefined substances to completed items, inside a solitary office. This upward mix smoothes out the creation interaction, lessens strategic intricacies, and empowers more tight command over quality and expenses.

Gigafactory 1, situated close to Reno, Nevada, fills in as the model for resulting Gigafactories. The office's emphasis on lithium-particle battery creation, including cells, modules, and packs, mirrors Musk's obligation to tending to the center test of battery adaptability. By solidifying the whole battery creation chain under one rooftop, Tesla intended to advance proficiency, improve quality control, and accomplish cost decreases that would convert into additional reasonable electric vehicles.

The execution of Gigafactories includes the use of state of the art producing advances. Robotization and mechanical technology assume a critical part in accomplishing accuracy and proficiency at scale. The joining of Industry 4.0 standards, described by the utilization of advanced innovations in assembling processes, guarantees that Gigafactories are outfitted with cutting edge apparatus and information driven dynamic abilities. This hug of cutting edge innovations lines up with Musk's general objective of pushing the limits of advancement and innovation.

The scale accomplished by Gigafactories is uncommon in the battery fabricating scene. Gigafactory, endless supply of its development stages, became one of the biggest assembling offices universally, covering over 5.5 million square feet. This monster scope considers the development of batteries in amounts that were beforehand unbelievable, adding to a huge decrease in the expense each kilowatt-hour. The economies of scale acknowledged through Gigafactories play had a urgent impact in reshaping the financial matters of electric vehicles and energy stockpiling arrangements.

The effect of accomplishing scale and productivity in battery creation reaches out past electric vehicles to incorporate energy stockpiling arrangements. Batteries are urgent parts in putting away energy created from sustainable sources, for example, sun oriented and wind. The adaptability accomplished through Gigafactories empowers the development of enormous limit batteries reasonable for private, business, and utility-scale energy capacity applications. This adaptability in battery creation lines up with the more extensive pattern of coordinating sustainable power into existing power frameworks.

Gigafactories are intended to help the development of a different scope of battery items, from the Powerwall for private energy stockpiling to the Megapack for utility-scale projects. The Powerwall, with its minimal plan, is reasonable for property holders trying to store overabundance energy created from sunlight based chargers for use during times of low daylight or high energy interest. Then again, the Megapack, with its enormous limit, is equipped towards giving framework scale energy capacity answers for upgrade the strength and dependability of energy networks.

The progress of accomplishing scale and proficiency in battery creation is clear in the effect on the electric vehicle market. Perhaps of the main result has been the expanded moderateness of electric vehicles, especially exemplified by Tesla's Model 3. The Model 3, situated as a mass-market electric vehicle, has turned into a worldwide success, exhibiting the potential for boundless reception of electric vehicles when cost boundaries are relieved. This change in moderateness lines up with Musk's more extensive mission of speeding up the world's progress to maintainable energy.

Gigafactory Shanghai, Tesla's office in China, addresses an essential development of the Gigafactory model. Functional since late 2019, Gigafactory Shanghai centers around the development of the Model 3 and the Model Y for the Chinese market. The choice to lay out a Gigafactory in China mirrors the country's status as the biggest electric vehicle market worldwide. The confined creation in China assists Tesla with alleviating import duties, diminish transporting costs, and adjust to provincial requests. Gigafactory Shanghai fills in as a demonstration of the versatility and versatility of the Gigafactory model to meet the particular necessities of key business sectors.

Gigafactory Berlin, as of now under development in Grünheide, Germany, is one more huge achievement in the worldwide extension of the Gigafactory idea. The office is supposed to deliver batteries, battery packs, and powertrains, notwithstanding electric vehicles. Gigafactory Berlin is decisively situated to take care of the European market, lining up with the landmass' push towards electric portability and sustainable power. The development of Gigafactory Berlin highlights Musk's obligation to confinement and responsiveness to territorial requests.

Gigafactory Texas, reported in 2020 and situated in Austin, Texas, is intended to be an assembling center for Tesla's electric vehicles, including the Cybertruck. The choice to lay out Gigafactory Texas mirrors Musk's acknowledgment of the essential significance of the U.S. market and the potential for electric vehicles in the pickup truck fragment. Gigafactory Texas addresses a significant interest in the U.S. auto area and adds to the reshaping of the country's auto scene.

The Gigafactory model plays had a crucial impact in reclassifying the electric vehicle market as well as the energy stockpiling industry. The versatility and effectiveness accomplished through Gigafactories add to the steadiness and flexibility of energy matrices by working with the development of enormous scope energy capacity arrangements. The Megapack, intended for utility-scale projects, addresses a stage towards matrix scale energy capacity. By sending Megapacks, energy suppliers can store abundance energy produced during times of low interest and delivery it during top interest, improving the effectiveness and unwavering quality of energy frameworks.

While the accomplishments in accomplishing scale and proficiency in battery creation are exemplary, the Gigafactory model isn't without its difficulties and discussions. One of the outstanding difficulties is the ecological effect related with the quick organization and huge size of Gigafactories. Concerns connected with water utilization, deforestation, and likely effects on biodiversity have been subjects of examination and administrative difficulties. Musk's reaction to these worries mirrors a continuous obligation to address natural contemplations and work towards manageable assembling rehearses.

The reconciliation of environmentally friendly power sources in Gigafactories, for example, sun oriented and wind power, is a stage towards moderating the natural effect. Gigafactory 1, for example, consolidates sun powered chargers on its rooftop and encompassing regions, adding to a decreased carbon impression. Musk's accentuation on supportability and natural obligation mirrors a more extensive consciousness of the need to adjust the groundbreaking effect of Gigafactories with environmental contemplations.

All in all, accomplishing scale and effectiveness in battery creation, as exemplified by the Gigafactory model, is significant for the progression of electric vehicles and sustainable power stockpiling arrangements.

Elon Musk's vision of tending to the expense difficulties related with batteries has brought about extraordinary changes in the electric vehicle market and the more extensive progress to manageable energy. The economies of scale acknowledged through Gigafactories have made electric vehicles more reasonable as well as situated energy capacity arrangements as basic parts in the progress to sustainable power. As Gigafactories proceed to develop and multiply worldwide, their effect on ventures, economies, and the climate will be a characterizing factor in forming an additional practical and charged future.

The Gigafactory Upset addresses an extraordinary change in the worldwide assembling scene, especially in the creation of electric vehicles (EVs) and environmentally friendly power advancements. This peculiarity is encapsulated by the development and activity of gigafactories — uber scale offices intended for the large scale manufacturing of batteries, which are the soul of EVs and fundamental for putting away environmentally friendly power.

At the core of this insurgency is the rising interest for supportable and clean energy answers for battle environmental change. The criticalness to decrease fossil fuel byproducts has driven a flood in the reception of electric vehicles, pushing automakers to put vigorously in gigafactories to increase battery creation. The dramatic development of the electric vehicle market, combined with progressions in environmentally friendly power stockpiling advancements, has catalyzed the foundation of gigafactories as crucial centers for development and large scale manufacturing.

One of the vital participants in this upheaval is Tesla, drove by visionary business person Elon Musk. Tesla's Gigafactories have become inseparable from state of the art innovation and have set new norms for effectiveness and scale in battery creation. The Gigafactory in Nevada, frequently alluded to as Gigafactory 1, is a perfect representation of this pattern. It remains as a demonstration of the effect a solitary office can have on the whole auto and energy areas.

The gigafactory model isn't selective to Tesla, as other significant automakers and tech organizations are hustling to lay out their own uber offices. Organizations like Volkswagen, General Engines, and CATL (Contemporary Amperex Innovation Co. Restricted) are effective financial planning billions of dollars to develop gigafactories across the globe. This worldwide multiplication mirrors the acknowledgment of batteries as a basic part in the change to a supportable, low-carbon future.

Past electric vehicles, gigafactories assume a vital part in propelling energy stockpiling arrangements, tending to the discontinuity of environmentally friendly power sources, for example, sun based and wind. The capacity to store energy at an enormous scope is fundamental for accomplishing a dependable and strong lattice. Accordingly, gigafactories are changing the auto business as well as forming the fate of the whole energy biological system.

The monetary effect of the gigafactory unrest reaches out past the organizations straightforwardly associated with assembling. Gigafactories make occupations, animate neighborhood economies, and add to the improvement of encompassing networks. The gradually expanding influence of these super offices is felt in different areas, from development and planned operations to innovation and exploration.

Additionally, the gigafactory transformation is driving development in battery innovation. Innovative work endeavors are centered around improving energy thickness, expanding battery duration, and diminishing expenses. Leap forwards here are significant for making electric vehicles more reasonable and open to a more extensive populace, in this manner speeding up the worldwide progress to maintainable transportation.

As gigafactories multiply, worries about the ecological effect of battery creation have come to the very front. The extraction and handling of natural substances, like lithium, cobalt, and nickel, bring up issues about the maintainability of the whole store network. Endeavors to foster more practical battery sciences and reusing innovations are in progress, expecting to moderate the natural impression of gigafactories and the electric vehicle industry all in all.

Government strategies and guidelines assume a critical part in forming the direction of the gigafactory unrest. Motivations and appropriations given by states overall empower interest in sustainable power and electric vehicle creation. Policymakers perceive the capability of gigafactories to drive financial development, diminish ozone depleting substance emanations, and position their nations as pioneers in the perfect energy progress.

The international ramifications of the gigafactory insurgency are likewise significant. The race for mechanical predominance in electric vehicles and energy stockpiling has turned into a critical part of worldwide rivalry. Nations and organizations that effectively set up a good foundation for themselves as pioneers in gigafactory innovation gain a competitive edge in the new energy scene, impacting financial and political elements on a worldwide scale.

In any case, challenges loom not too far off. The multifaceted store network of battery creation, combined with the international pressures encompassing the extraction of basic minerals, presents dangers to the strength of the gigafactory transformation. The business should wrestle with issues of asset shortage, moral obtaining, and international contentions to guarantee a manageable and impartial future for the gigafactory biological system.

All in all, the gigafactory transformation denotes a change in perspective in the manner we produce and consume energy. As the world wrestles with the dire need to progress to a low-carbon economy, gigafactories arise as impetuses for change.

These uber offices are reshaping the auto and energy ventures as well as impacting the worldwide economy, legislative issues, and the climate. The excursion towards a supportable future is complicatedly attached to the achievement and development of the gigafactory unrest, making it a significant section in the continuous story of human advancement.

Chapter 5

Innovations in Battery Technology

In the constant quest for propelling innovation, perhaps of the most basic wilderness has been the advancement of battery innovation. Throughout recent many years, batteries have become universal in our regular routines, driving everything from little electronic gadgets to electric vehicles and environmentally friendly power frameworks. The requirement for more effective, feasible, and high-limit energy capacity arrangements has prompted a flood in developments in battery innovation, reshaping the scene of different enterprises and pushing the limits of what was once imagined.

One of the huge leap forwards as of late has been the coming of strong state batteries. Conventional lithium-particle batteries, while effective, have constraints concerning energy thickness, wellbeing, and generally speaking execution. Strong state batteries address these worries by supplanting the fluid or gel electrolytes in regular batteries with strong electrolyte materials. This not just works on the security of the batteries by taking out the gamble of spillage or burning yet in addition considers higher energy thickness and quicker charging times.

The utilization of strong state batteries stretches out past purchaser hardware, influencing the electric vehicle (EV) industry. Electric vehicles have acquired fame as a cleaner and more maintainable option in contrast to conventional fuel controlled vehicles. Be that as it may, the restricted reach and long charging times have been industrious difficulties. Strong state batteries vow to change the EV area by giving higher energy thickness, empowering longer ranges on a solitary charge, and fundamentally lessening the time required for re-energizing. This advancement is an essential move toward making electric vehicles more viable and interesting to a more extensive crowd.

Besides, the combination of computerized reasoning (simulated intelligence) in battery the executives frameworks plays had an essential impact in upgrading battery execution and expanding their life expectancy. Simulated intelligence calculations break down ongoing information, including temperature, charge/release cycles, and use designs, to come to canny conclusions about how the battery ought to be worked. This upgrades the productivity of energy stockpiling as well as forestalls issues like overheating and corruption. Accordingly, the life expectancy of batteries is delayed, decreasing the recurrence of substitutions and adding to generally speaking maintainability.

In the domain of sustainable power, matrix scale energy capacity has turned into a point of convergence for guaranteeing the dependability and solidness of force frameworks. The discontinuous idea of sustainable sources like sun oriented and wind power presents difficulties to keeping a reliable energy supply. High level battery innovations, including stream batteries and high level lithium-particle variations, are progressively being conveyed to store abundance energy produced during times of high sustainable result. These put away energy stores can then be released during seasons of low sustainable age, successfully adjusting the network and guaranteeing a consistent power supply.

The reconciliation of nanotechnology has likewise assumed a urgent part in upgrading the presentation of batteries. Nanomaterials, for example, nanowires and nanotubes, show interesting electrical and mechanical properties that can be utilized to further develop energy capacity. For example, the utilization of nanomaterials in cathode configuration builds the surface region accessible for electrochemical responses, prompting higher energy stockpiling limits. Moreover, nanotechnology empowers the advancement of lightweight and adaptable batteries, opening up additional opportunities for wearable gadgets and different applications where conventional inflexible batteries are unrealistic.

Chasing after manageability, scientists are investigating elective materials for battery creation to lessen dependence on scant and naturally unsafe assets. For example, lithium, a vital part in numerous batteries, isn't just costly yet in addition presents natural worries because of its extraction cycle.

Researchers are effectively examining elective materials, for example, sodium and potassium, which are more plentiful and harmless to the ecosystem.This shift towards supportable materials lines up with the more extensive worldwide push for eco-accommodating advancements and practices.

Past the actual parts of batteries, progressions in assembling strategies have smoothed out creation processes, diminishing expenses and further developing adaptability. Procedures, for example, 3D printing and roll-to-move fabricating have empowered the quick and savvy creation of batteries with hand crafts. This not just works with the production of batteries customized to explicit applications yet additionally speeds up the speed of advancement by permitting scientists to model and test new plans all the more proficiently.

The Web of Things (IoT) has additionally impelled the development of battery innovation by encouraging an interest for minimized, dependable, and effective power hotspots for a heap of associated gadgets. From shrewd home gadgets to modern sensors, the requirement for batteries that can give broadened functional existence without successive substitutions is vital. Scaling down of batteries, combined with enhancements in energy thickness, has made ready for another age of IoT gadgets that can work for broadened periods on a solitary battery charge.

In the clinical field, the advancement of biocompatible batteries has opened additional opportunities for implantable clinical gadgets. Customary batteries present provokes when utilized in inserts because of their size, restricted life expectancy, and possible poisonousness. Biocompatible batteries, frequently controlled by biofuel cells or utilizing materials that the body can securely process, offer a manageable and safe power hotspot for clinical inserts. This development can possibly reform the field of clinical inserts, empowering longer-enduring and more adaptable gadgets for checking and treating different medical issue.

As the world changes towards electric versatility, the charging foundation is a basic part of the general environment. The development of remote charging innovation is tending to a portion of the difficulties related with regular charging strategies. Remote charging wipes out the requirement for actual connectors, giving a more helpful and consistent experience for clients. Electric vehicles outfitted with remote charging capacities can just stop over a charging cushion, and the exchange of energy happens through electromagnetic fields. This works on the charging system as well as lessens the mileage on physical charging connectors, adding to the life span of the charging foundation.

The push for supportable energy arrangements has prompted the investigation of creative ideas like second-life batteries. As batteries arrive at the finish of their life in electric vehicles or different applications, they might in any case hold a huge piece of their unique limit. Rather than reusing or discarding these batteries, they can be reused for auxiliary applications, like fixed energy capacity. This boosts the worth of the batteries as well as decreases the natural effect of removal. Second-life batteries act as a halfway move toward the in general lifecycle of batteries, stretching out their helpfulness and adding to a more round economy.

In the journey for additional harmless to the ecosystem choices, analysts are likewise exploring the capability of natural batteries. Dissimilar to traditional batteries that utilization metal-based terminals and electrolytes, natural batteries influence carbon-based materials. These materials are more bountiful, harmless to the ecosystem, and posture less dangers concerning asset shortage and removal. While natural batteries are still in the beginning phases of improvement, they hold guarantee for giving a greener option in contrast to conventional battery advances.

The idea of energy collecting, wherein limited quantities of energy are caught from encompassing sources, is building up some decent forward movement as a reciprocal way to deal with customary battery innovation. This includes catching energy from sources like daylight, vibrations, or temperature differentials and changing over it into electrical power. While energy collecting alone may not be adequate for high-energy-request applications, it can essentially expand the battery duration of low-power gadgets and sensors. This development is especially significant in applications where successive battery substitutions are unreasonable or exorbitant.

The worldwide push towards decarbonization and diminishing dependence on petroleum products has sped up the reception of electric airplane. Batteries assume a vital part in driving electric flying, and headways in battery innovation are instrumental in conquering the difficulties related with the energy thickness expected for long-range flights. High-limit batteries fit for giving supported capacity to expanded periods are fundamental for the feasibility of electric airplane. The improvement of lightweight materials and high level warm administration frameworks further adds to the productivity and wellbeing of electric flying.

All in all, the scene of battery innovation is ceaselessly developing, driven by the twin objectives of proficiency and maintainability. From strong state batteries and man-made reasoning driven administration frameworks to nanotechnology and the investigation of elective materials, the advancements in battery innovation are reshaping ventures and affecting the manner in which we live, work, and move. As we look toward the future, the combination of these headways guarantees an existence where energy capacity isn't just more productive and economical yet additionally assumes a significant part in tending to worldwide difficulties, for example, environmental change and the progress to a perfect energy future.

5.1 . Unveiling the "4680" Battery Cell

The energy scene is going through an extraordinary shift, with an emphasis on economical and proficient answers for power the world's developing requests. At the bleeding edge of this insurgency is the improvement of cutting edge battery advances, and one of the main ongoing forward leaps is the disclosing of the "4680" battery cell. This creative battery configuration addresses a jump forward in energy capacity capacities and is ready to significantly affect enterprises going from electric vehicles (EVs) to sustainable power frameworks.

Tesla, the electric vehicle and clean energy organization drove by Elon Musk, presented the "4680" battery cell during its Battery Day occasion in 2020. Named after its aspects - 46 millimeters in breadth and 80 millimeters in level - the "4680" cell is a takeoff from the conventional round and hollow cells that have been common in the business. The bigger structure element of the "4680" cell brings a few benefits, basically revolved around further developed energy thickness, warm administration, and by and large execution.

One of the vital advantages of the "4680" cell is its higher energy thickness, which alludes to how much energy a battery can store for every unit of volume. The bigger size considers more dynamic materials, like cathodes and anodes, to be pressed into the cell, expanding the general energy stockpiling limit. This means batteries that can convey more power and broaden the scope of electric vehicles without a huge expansion in weight or size. The higher energy thickness of the "4680" cell is a basic figure tending to the constraints of flow battery innovation and driving the broad reception of electric vehicles.

Warm administration is another region where the "4680" cell exhibits remarkable upgrades. Productive warm administration is critical for battery security and execution, especially sought after circumstances, for example, quick charging and supported high-power yield. The bigger size of the "4680" cell considers a more viable conveyance of intensity inside the cell, lessening the gamble of overheating and working on in general warm steadiness. This is a critical headway in guaranteeing the security and dependability of electric vehicles, as warm issues have been a worry in the improvement of superior execution batteries.

Besides, the "4680" cell includes another tabless plan, dispensing with the conventional tab that interfaces the cell's anode to the outside terminals. This plan development improves the cell's power yield by giving a more straightforward way to electrons, decreasing interior opposition and empowering quicker charge and release rates. The tabless plan works on the phone's presentation as well as improves on the assembling system, adding to cost effectiveness and adaptability.

The assembling system itself is a significant part of the "4680" cell. Tesla has carried out creative assembling procedures, including a consistent creation process known as "bread roll tin" or "cutout" producing. In conventional battery creation, anodes are regularly made in sheets and afterward cut into the ideal shape. The constant assembling approach of the "4680" cell includes moving up the terminal material, like moving up a rug, bringing about a more smoothed out and practical interaction. This approach further develops effectiveness as well as decreases waste and brings down the general creation expenses of the battery cells.

The presentation of the "4680" battery cell has expansive ramifications for the electric vehicle market. Tesla expects to coordinate these cells into its vehicles, beginning with the Tesla Model Y delivered at the Gigafactory in Berlin.

The expanded energy thickness, combined with progressions in warm administration and assembling productivity, vows to convey electric vehicles with longer ranges, quicker charging times, and improved generally speaking execution. This, thusly, adds to stalling boundaries to EV reception, making electric vehicles more interesting to a more extensive crowd and speeding up the progress to managcable transportation.

Past electric vehicles, the "4680" battery cell has applications in fixed energy capacity. As the world endeavors to coordinate more environmentally friendly power sources into the power matrix, productive energy stockpiling arrangements become progressively basic. The "4680" cell's higher energy thickness and further developed warm qualities make it appropriate for fixed capacity frameworks, empowering better incorporation of sustainable power sources like sunlight based and wind power. Tesla's Megapack, a huge scope fixed energy capacity arrangement, is supposed to profit from the headways presented by the "4680" cell, giving network steadiness and working with the progress to a more reasonable energy foundation.

The revealing of the "4680" battery cell has additionally ignited interest and coordinated effort across the car and energy ventures. Tesla has reported plans to supply these cells to different automakers, opening up open doors for more extensive reception of cutting edge battery innovation past Tesla's own vehicles. This cooperative methodology lines up with the more extensive objective of tending to environmental change and advancing maintainable practices across the business. The sharing of mechanical headways can facilitate the turn of events and organization of electric vehicles on a worldwide scale, adding to a cleaner and all the more harmless to the ecosystem transportation biological system.

Notwithstanding its effect on electric vehicles and fixed stockpiling, the "4680" battery cell has suggestions for matrix scale energy capacity. The capacity to store a lot of energy proficiently is vital for adjusting the discontinuous idea of environmentally friendly power sources and guaranteeing a dependable power supply. The "4680" cell's high energy thickness and vigorous warm administration make it a promising possibility for huge scope matrix capacity projects, further supporting the change to an environmentally friendly power future.

Difficulties and contemplations go with the broad reception of the "4680" battery cell. Similarly as with any mechanical advancement, there are inquiries regarding the adaptability of creation to fulfill the developing need for electric vehicles and energy stockpiling arrangements. Tesla's Gigafactories, intended for high-volume creation of batteries, assume a significant part in tending to this test. The outcome of the "4680" cell will depend on its specialized benefits as well as on the capacity to increase creation proficiently to meet the aggressive targets set by Tesla and the more extensive industry.

Natural supportability is another basic angle that requires consideration. While electric vehicles offer a cleaner option in contrast to conventional gas powered motor vehicles, the creation and removal of batteries raise ecological worries.

The mining and extraction of unrefined components, like lithium and cobalt, are related with ecological effects, including natural surroundings obliteration and water contamination. Endeavors to foster more manageable and moral obtaining rehearses for these materials, as well as progressions in reusing advancements, are fundamental for limiting the natural impression of battery creation.

All in all, the divulging of the "4680" battery cell denotes a critical achievement in the development of battery innovation. Its bigger structure factor, higher energy thickness, worked on warm administration, and inventive assembling procedures address a far reaching way to deal with tending to the difficulties of current battery innovation. As the car and energy ventures progressively focus on manageability and productivity, the "4680" cell arises as a key empowering influence for the far and wide reception of electric vehicles, sustainable power frameworks, and matrix scale energy capacity. The effect of this advancement reaches out past individual organizations, encouraging cooperation and speeding up the worldwide progress to a cleaner and more practical energy future.

5.2. Advancing Energy Density and Manufacturing Efficiency

In the consistently advancing scene of energy stockpiling, the quest for higher energy thickness and assembling productivity remains as a foundation in the improvement of cutting edge battery advances. As the interest for electric vehicles (EVs), environmentally friendly power sources, and lattice scale capacity keeps on developing, specialists and industry pioneers are steadily enhancing to defeat the constraints of flow battery frameworks. This drive for progress envelops upgrades in energy thickness, the core of battery execution, as well as improvements in assembling cycles to increase creation proficiently and reasonably.

Energy thickness, a key measurement in battery innovation, alludes to how much energy a battery can store for each unit of volume or weight. It straightforwardly influences the scope of electric vehicles, the productivity of convenient electronic gadgets, and the suitability of fixed energy capacity arrangements. Headways in energy thickness contribute not exclusively to the improvement of existing applications yet in addition to the development of potential outcomes in arising advances.

Lithium-particle batteries have been the workhorse of convenient gadgets and electric vehicles for quite a long time, however their energy thickness has arrived at a level, requiring the investigation of elective sciences and plans. One promising road is the improvement of strong state batteries, which supplant the fluid or gel electrolytes in conventional lithium-particle batteries with strong materials. Strong state batteries offer the potential for higher energy thickness, expanded security, and longer cycle life.

The shortfall of fluid electrolytes in strong state batteries decreases the gamble of spillage and warm out of control, tending to somewhere safe and secure worries related with customary lithium-particle batteries.

Moreover, the utilization of strong electrolytes considers the consolidation of lithium metal anodes, which have a higher energy thickness contrasted with customary graphite anodes. This underlying change inside the battery engineering brings about expanded generally speaking energy stockpiling limit.

Organizations and examination foundations all around the world are putting resources into strong state battery innovative work to carry this innovation to business feasibility. The auto business, specifically, sees strong state batteries as a distinct advantage for electric vehicles. The commitment of expanded energy thickness and security lines up with the yearnings for longer driving reaches and quicker charging times, tending to basic variables in the far and wide reception of electric transportation.

Past strong state batteries, lithium-sulfur (Li-S) batteries have additionally arisen as a competitor for essentially higher energy thickness. Dissimilar to customary lithium-particle batteries, Li-S batteries use sulfur as the cathode material, which isn't just bountiful yet in addition has a high hypothetical limit. The mix of lithium and sulfur might possibly offer energy densities a few times higher than current lithium-particle innovation.

Notwithstanding, Li-S batteries face difficulties, for example, the "van impact," where polysulfide particles can relocate between the anode and cathode, prompting limit misfortune and decreased execution over the long run. Specialists are effectively chipping away at relieving these difficulties through imaginative materials and plans. In the event that effective, Li-S batteries could reform energy capacity, especially in applications where it is principal to boost energy thickness.

Pair with headways in energy thickness, an equal spotlight on assembling productivity is essential to satisfy the developing need for energy capacity arrangements. The assembling system essentially impacts the expense, versatility, and natural effect of battery creation.

Conventional battery fabricating includes numerous means, including cathode readiness, cell gathering, and electrolyte filling, each requiring cautious accuracy. Mechanization plays had a significant impact in smoothing out these cycles, decreasing human mistake, and expanding creation effectiveness. Present day fabricating offices, like Tesla's Gigafactories, use progressed mechanization to gather battery cells at scale, adding to cost decrease and creation speed.

Besides, persistent assembling procedures are acquiring conspicuousness in the mission for productivity. As opposed to collecting batteries in clumps, ceaseless assembling considers a consistent, continuous cycle, like how items are created in mechanical production systems. This approach wipes out the requirement for tedious halfway advances, lessening creation costs and expanding in general throughput.

Chasing after additional feasible and harmless to the ecosystem rehearses, analysts are investigating greener assembling techniques. Water-based terminal assembling is one such model. Conventional anode fabricating processes include the utilization of poisonous solvents, presenting ecological and wellbeing chances. Water-based processes take out the requirement for unsafe solvents, decreasing the natural effect and guaranteeing a more secure work space for assembling staff.

As well as refining fabricating processes, the investigation of elective materials for battery parts adds to both effectiveness and manageability. The mission for more bountiful and eco-accommodating materials is reshaping the scene of battery innovation. Silicon, for example, is being explored as an option in contrast to graphite in the structure of anodes. Silicon has a higher hypothetical limit with respect to lithium ingestion, possibly prompting batteries with expanded energy thickness.

In any case, silicon goes through critical volume changes during charging and releasing, which can cause mechanical pressure and compromise the underlying uprightness of the battery. To address this test, analysts are creating silicon composites and nanostructured materials that can oblige the volume changes all the more successfully, making ready for the pragmatic execution of silicon anodes in business batteries.

In the cathode domain, analysts are investigating different materials, including nickel-rich cathodes, to upgrade the energy thickness of batteries. Nickel-rich cathodes offer higher energy stockpiling limits, however they likewise face difficulties connected with warm soundness and life expectancy. Developments in cathode plan and the consolidation of defensive coatings expect to moderate these difficulties, making nickel-rich cathodes a reasonable choice for cutting edge batteries.

The joining of man-made reasoning (simulated intelligence) and AI (ML) into battery fabricating processes addresses one more outskirts in propelling productivity. Man-made intelligence calculations can examine immense measures of information continuously, enhancing creation boundaries to work on the quality and execution of batteries. From anode sythesis to cell gathering, artificial intelligence driven assembling guarantees accuracy and consistency, at last prompting more significant returns and lower creation costs.

Battery the board frameworks (BMS) improved by computer based intelligence are instrumental in streamlining the exhibition and life expectancy of batteries. These frameworks consistently screen different boundaries, like temperature, voltage, and charge/release cycles, and utilize the information to arrive at smart conclusions about how the battery ought to be worked. This boosts energy capacity effectiveness as well as adds to the security and life span of batteries.

With regards to electric vehicles, simulated intelligence controlled BMS assumes a pivotal part in prescient upkeep. By examining information from sensors implanted in the vehicle and the battery pack, artificial intelligence calculations can expect possible issues before they become basic, considering proactive support and limiting free time. This prescient methodology is especially important for the unwavering quality and cost-viability of electric vehicle armadas.

As the interest for energy capacity arrangements keeps on raising, reusing and reusing of batteries are becoming vital parts of a maintainable battery biological system. The materials utilized in batteries, including metals like lithium, cobalt, and nickel, are important and can be recuperated through reusing processes. This diminishes the natural effect of mining as well as mitigates worries about the accessibility of basic materials.

Developments in reusing advancements mean to proficiently remove materials from spent batteries more. Hydrometallurgical processes, for instance, utilize watery answers for specifically disintegrate and recuperate metals from battery parts. These cycles offer a cleaner and more asset proficient option in contrast to customary refining strategies, limiting waste and energy utilization.

Reusing of batteries is one more road for reasonable practices. Subsequent to arriving at the finish of their valuable life in electric vehicles, batteries might in any case hold a huge part of their ability. These "second-life" batteries can be reused for fixed energy capacity applications, broadening their convenience and lessening the requirement for new battery creation. This approach lines up with the standards of a round economy, where items and materials are reused, repaired, and reused to limit squander and expand asset effectiveness.

In the more extensive setting of a practical energy future, developments in energy capacity are firmly entwined with the development of environmentally friendly power sources. The irregular idea of sun based and wind power requires viable energy stockpiling answers for balance market interest on the network. Matrix scale energy capacity, empowered by cutting edge battery innovations, gives a system to putting away overabundance energy created during times of high inexhaustible result and delivering it during seasons of low age.

Redox stream batteries address a promising answer for framework scale energy capacity. Dissimilar to customary batteries with strong cathodes, redox stream batteries utilize fluid electrolytes put away in outer tanks. This plan takes into consideration decoupling of force and energy, empowering the free scaling of the battery's power and capacity limit. Redox stream batteries offer benefits concerning versatility, adaptability, and strength, making them appropriate for applications where an enormous scope, long-length energy capacity arrangement is required.

As energy stockpiling innovations keep on advancing, the reconciliation of batteries with arising advancements like the Web of Things (IoT) and 5G organizations opens new outskirts. Savvy matrices, empowered by cutting edge battery the executives frameworks and continuous information examination, take into consideration dynamic and responsive energy circulation. This degree of framework insight improves proficiency, dependability, and versatility, making ready for a more versatile and reasonable energy foundation.

All in all, the double spotlight on propelling energy thickness and assembling proficiency is pushing the battery innovation scene into another time. From strong state batteries and lithium-sulfur sciences to consistent assembling cycles and computer based intelligence driven streamlining, the advancements in battery innovation are reshaping ventures and affecting the direction of the worldwide change to economical energy. As these headways keep on unfurling, the collaboration between energy capacity, environmentally friendly power sources, and brilliant matrix innovations holds the way in to a future where dependable, clean, and proficient energy is open on a worldwide scale.

As of late, the field of battery innovation has seen wonderful advancements, reforming the manner in which we power our gadgets and vehicles. These headways have been driven by a mix of expanding interest for energy capacity arrangements, ecological worries, and the quest for more productive and maintainable power sources.

One of the critical areas of advancement in battery innovation has been the improvement of lithium-particle batteries. Since their business presentation in the mid 1990s, these batteries have turned into the standard power hotspot for a large number of uses, from cell phones and workstations to electric vehicles (EVs). The high energy thickness and generally light weight of lithium-particle batteries make them ideal for versatile electronic gadgets, empowering longer utilization times and decreasing the requirement for incessant re-energizing.

As the interest for electric vehicles has flooded, scientists and specialists have zeroed in on upgrading the presentation of lithium-particle batteries to meet the particular necessities of car applications. Endeavors have been made to increment energy thickness, broaden battery duration, and improve charging times. Developments in anode materials, like the utilization of silicon instead of graphite, have shown guarantee in helping the limit of lithium-particle batteries, tending to one of the critical restrictions of this innovation.

Past lithium-particle, scientists have been investigating elective battery sciences to defeat the restrictions of existing advancements. Strong state batteries, for instance, certainly stand out for their capability to offer higher energy thickness, further developed security, and longer life expectancy contrasted with customary lithium-particle batteries. By supplanting the fluid electrolyte with a strong material, strong state batteries mean to lessen the gamble of warm out of control and improve in general dependability, making them appealing for applications where wellbeing is a vital concern.

In the journey for maintainability, specialists are additionally examining the advancement of harmless to the ecosystem and savvy battery advances. One promising road is the investigation of materials past lithium, like sodium-particle batteries. Sodium, being more bountiful and more affordable than lithium, could give a more supportable option in contrast to huge scope energy capacity applications. While sodium-particle batteries are still in the beginning phases of improvement, they hold the possibility to assume a huge part in the change to more supportable energy frameworks.

Moreover, the coordination of environmentally friendly power sources, for example, sun based and wind power, into the electrical framework has prompted an expanded requirement for energy capacity arrangements prepared to do proficiently putting away and conveying power when these irregular sources are not free. High level battery innovations, including stream batteries and high level lead-corrosive batteries, are being investigated for their capacity to furnish network scale energy capacity with further developed effectiveness and dependability.

Chasing elite execution batteries, nanotechnology has arisen as a significant device for controlling materials at the nuclear and sub-atomic levels. Nanostructured materials can improve the electrical conductivity, surface region, and by and large execution of battery parts. For example, nanoscale coatings on terminals can work on their security and cycling execution, adding to longer-enduring and more proficient batteries.

The Web of Things (IoT) time has presented new difficulties and open doors for battery innovation. The multiplication of associated gadgets has spurred an interest for minimized, lightweight, and dependable batteries to drive sensors and other IoT gadgets. Scientists are investigating scaled down energy capacity arrangements, like microbatteries and meager film batteries, to meet the interesting necessities of IoT applications.

Progressions in battery the executives frameworks (BMS) have likewise assumed a urgent part in working on the general execution and security of batteries. BMS innovation empowers continuous observing of individual cells inside a battery pack, upgrading charging and releasing cycles to boost productivity and forestall issues, for example, cheating and overheating. The mix of savvy BMS frameworks in electric vehicles, for instance, upgrades the security and dependability of the whole energy stockpiling framework.

Notwithstanding mechanical developments, there is a developing spotlight on the reusing and maintainability of battery innovations. The far reaching reception of electric vehicles and sustainable power frameworks has raised worries about the natural effect of battery assembling and removal. Endeavors are being made to foster proficient reusing cycles to recuperate significant materials from utilized batteries and diminish the ecological impression of battery creation.

Government drives and guidelines are additionally molding the scene of battery innovation. Numerous nations are putting resources into innovative work to help the development of the battery business and advance the reception of electric vehicles. Motivators for battery reusing and natural guidelines in regards to the utilization of specific materials in batteries are driving makers to investigate more feasible practices.

As battery innovation keeps on advancing, the opportunities for advancement are immense. From working on the effectiveness and supportability of energy stockpiling to empowering the far and wide reception of electric vehicles, these headways have sweeping ramifications for our energy scene. The continuous joint effort between scientists, designers, and industry partners holds the way to opening the maximum capacity of battery innovation and introducing another time of perfect, dependable, and effective energy stockpiling arrangements.

Chapter 6

Vertical Integration and Scalability

In the steadily developing scene of business and innovation, the ideas of vertical reconciliation and versatility have become critical for associations endeavoring to keep an upper hand. These two interrelated ideas, however unmistakable in nature, assume a synergistic part in molding the achievement and maintainability of organizations in the 21st 100 years.

Vertical incorporation, at its center, alludes to the technique where an organization grows tasks by procuring or creating organizations are essential for its production network or dispersion organization. This can include moving either upstream or downstream in the creation cycle. Upstream incorporation includes securing providers or natural substance makers, while downstream combination includes gaining merchants or retailers.

The benefits of vertical reconciliation are diverse. One of the essential advantages lies in the potential for cost decrease. By bringing different phases of the creation cycle under the umbrella of a solitary element, economies of scale can be understood. This decreases exchange costs as well as improves functional productivity. The smoothing out of cycles inside the incorporated design frequently prompts further developed coordination and correspondence, limiting deferrals and mistakes.

In addition, vertical reconciliation gives associations more noteworthy command over their store network. This control is instrumental in guaranteeing the quality and dependability of data sources, consequently relieving the dangers related with outer providers. In a time where worldwide stockpile binds are defenseless to disturbances, like international strains, catastrophic events, or pandemics, the capacity to apply command over basic parts turns into a competitive edge.

Nonetheless, the way of vertical incorporation isn't without challenges. One prominent downside is the potential for diminished adaptability. Coordinated substances might find it trying to adjust rapidly to changes in the business climate or mechanical headways. Moreover, overseeing different tasks requires an alternate arrangement of abilities and capabilities, and associations should cautiously explore the intricacies to infer greatest advantages.

The connection between vertical reconciliation and versatility is multifaceted. Versatility, in a business setting, alludes to the capacity of a framework or cycle to deal with a developing measure of work, or its capability to be broadened to oblige that development. In this specific situation, vertical combination can essentially affect versatility, both emphatically and adversely.

On the positive side, vertical incorporation can improve versatility by giving a strong groundwork to development. At the point when an association controls different phases of its worth chain, it can all the more really scale its activities because of market requests. The coordinated construction considers a consistent expansion underway limit, as the whole production network is under the domain of a solitary element. This can be especially worthwhile in businesses where quick versatility is critical, like innovation and web based business.

Besides, vertical joining can add to adaptability by cultivating advancement. With a comprehensive perspective on the creation interaction, associations are better situated to distinguish regions for development and carry out imaginative arrangements. This ceaseless development upgrades productivity as well as prepares the association to scale its tasks in an economical way.

In any case, the connection between vertical combination and versatility isn't clear 100% of the time. Now and again, over the top incorporation can prevent versatility. Unbending nature inside a coordinated construction might make it trying to adjust to changing economic situations or embrace new innovations. The very includes that make vertical incorporation alluring, like control and coordination, can become obstacles when the requirement for nimbleness and adaptability emerges.

As organizations explore the perplexing territory of vertical combination and versatility, innovation arises as a basic empowering influence. In the 21st 100 years, the advanced unrest has reshaped the business scene, giving new devices and philosophies that rethink how associations approach coordination and adaptability.

The approach of cutting edge information investigation, man-made brainpower, and AI has engaged associations to separate significant bits of knowledge from gigantic datasets. This capacity is especially pertinent with regards to vertical coordination, where understanding and enhancing different phases of the store network can fundamentally affect proficiency and cost-adequacy. Prescient investigation, for example, empowers associations to gauge request all the more precisely, working with better preparation and asset distribution.

Besides, innovation assumes a significant part in improving versatility. Distributed computing, specifically, has upset the manner in which organizations scale their activities. The versatility inborn in cloud administrations permits associations to grow their framework and capacities on-request, without the requirement for critical forthright interests in actual equipment. This adaptability adjusts consistently with the unique idea of present day business conditions.

Chasing vertical coordination and adaptability, associations should likewise wrestle with the goals of supportability. As the worldwide local area defies the difficulties of environmental change and natural debasement, organizations are under expanding strain to take on rehearses that focus on ecological obligation.

Vertical combination, when drawn nearer in view of maintainability, can add to a more eco-accommodating store network. By applying command over the whole presentation process, associations can carry out naturally cognizant practices at each stage. This might incorporate the utilization of supportable unrefined components, energy-productive assembling processes, and capable waste administration. Such practices line up with moral and natural contemplations as well as resound decidedly with buyers who focus on maintainability.

Essentially, versatility in a practical setting includes the capacity to extend tasks without compromising natural honesty. Innovation, by and by, assumes an essential part in this situation. The combination of environmentally friendly power sources, the reception of roundabout economy standards, and the execution of eco-accommodating advances all add to the double objectives of versatility and manageability.

With regards to vertical incorporation, the accentuation on supportability reaches out past ecological worries to envelop social and moral aspects. Associations are progressively considered responsible for the functioning circumstances in their stockpile chains, and vertical joining gives a way to uphold moral principles across the whole presentation process. This includes guaranteeing fair work rehearses as well as advancing variety, value, and incorporation at all levels of the coordinated construction.

The crossing point of vertical reconciliation, adaptability, innovation, and manageability highlights the complicated snare of contemplations that organizations should explore in the 21st 100 years. Finding some kind of harmony requires a comprehensive methodology that considers the extraordinary elements of every industry, the developing assumptions for shoppers, and the more extensive cultural and natural setting.

As associations wrestle with these intricacies, key foreknowledge turns into an important resource. Expecting future patterns and disturbances permits organizations to situate themselves proactively, whether as far as upward mix to tie down their stock chains or adaptability to fulfill developing business sector needs.

This proactive position is worked with by the constant observing of mechanical headways, administrative changes, and changes in purchaser inclinations.

All in all, the assembly of vertical mix, versatility, innovation, and manageability shapes the direction of organizations in the 21st 100 years. While vertical coordination offers benefits as far as cost control, inventory network versatility, and quality affirmation, its effect on adaptability is nuanced and dependent upon the flexibility of the incorporated construction. Innovation arises as a basic empowering influence, giving the devices and capacities to enhance both vertical combination and versatility.

In this perplexing scene, the basic of supportability adds a moral and natural aspect to business techniques. Associations that effectively explore this multi-layered territory are ready to flourish in the present as well as to adjust and develop despite future difficulties. The excursion towards ideal vertical mix and versatility is a dynamic and continuous interaction, requiring spryness, development, and an unflinching obligation to moral and feasible practices.

6.1. Strategic Importance of Vertical Integration

In the perplexing embroidery of current business, the essential significance of vertical reconciliation stands apart as a unique power that shapes the cutthroat scene across different ventures. Vertical joining, an essential methodology where an organization broadens its impact over different phases of the store network, has shown to be a basic calculate accomplishing maintainable development, functional effectiveness, and upper hand.

One of the essential upper hands of vertical reconciliation lies in its capacity to upgrade cost control. By incorporating different phases of the creation cycle, from unrefined substance procurement to circulation, an organization can smooth out its tasks and lessen costs. This is accomplished through economies of scale, as the incorporated construction considers mass buying of data sources, proficient utilization of assets, and concentrated administration of creation processes.

Besides, vertical reconciliation gives a safeguard against inventory network interruptions. In a globalized and interconnected world, supply binds are powerless to different dangers, including international pressures, catastrophic events, and pandemics. Organizations that are upward coordinated have more prominent command over their stock chains, permitting them to answer all the more really to unexpected difficulties. This control mitigates the dangers related with outside providers and gives a degree of flexibility that is especially significant in the midst of emergency.

The essential significance of vertical reconciliation stretches out to the domain of value control. With command over different phases of the creation cycle, an organization can guarantee the consistency and nature of its items or administrations.

Here accuracy and unwavering quality are fundamental, like aviation, car, and drugs. By supervising each step from origination to conveyance, associations can maintain severe quality principles and fabricate a standing for greatness on the lookout.

Vertical joining likewise assumes an essential part in cultivating development. At the point when an organization controls different features of its worth chain, it acquires a complete comprehension of the whole presentation process. This knowledge empowers associations to recognize regions for development, execute imaginative arrangements, and adjust rapidly to changing business sector requests. The coordinated design works with a culture of ceaseless improvement and development, situating the organization as a dynamic and responsive player in the business.

Besides, vertical mix adds to vital separation. In business sectors immersed with comparable items or administrations, separation is a critical driver of upper hand.

Vertical combination permits organizations to offer novel incentives by controlling parts of their business that rivals may not. This could include restrictive admittance to explicit assets, exclusive innovations, or an in an upward direction adjusted client experience. Such separation upgrades market seriousness as well as lays out obstructions to passage for possible contenders.

With regards to vital significance, vertical mix likewise impacts evaluating methodologies. By controlling creation expenses and lessening conditions on outside providers, organizations can practice more noteworthy command over evaluating. This can prompt more cutthroat evaluating on the lookout or the capacity to keep up with greater costs for separated and premium items. The adaptability to adjust evaluating systems in light of market elements is an essential switch that can be used really through vertical mix.

Nonetheless, the essential significance of vertical mix isn't without its difficulties. One of the key contemplations is the harmony among reconciliation and adaptability. While vertical joining gives control and effectiveness, it can likewise bring unbending nature into the authoritative design. This unbending nature might make it moving for organizations to adjust quickly to changes in the business climate, mechanical progressions, or changes in purchaser inclinations. Finding some kind of harmony is significant to bridle the advantages of coordination without forfeiting the dexterity expected to flourish in unique business sectors.

One more test is the intricacy of overseeing assorted tasks. Vertical mix includes directing a scope of exercises, from obtainment to circulation, and requires different ranges of abilities and capabilities. Viable administration of these different capabilities requests a comprehensive methodology, with a sharp comprehension of each functional feature. Inability to deal with this intricacy can prompt failures and functional difficulties that might counterbalance the advantages of coordination.

The essential significance of vertical reconciliation is additionally affected by outer factors like administrative conditions and market elements. In certain ventures, administrative imperatives might restrict the degree to which an organization can upward coordinate. Antitrust regulations, for instance, may force limitations on monopolistic works on, influencing how much an organization have some control over different phases of the inventory network. Moreover, economic situations and client inclinations can develop, requiring a persistent reassessment of the incorporated system to line up with evolving elements.

As innovation keeps on rethinking enterprises, the essential significance of vertical coordination converges with the abilities of advanced change. The reconciliation of trend setting innovations, for example, man-made reasoning, information examination, and the Web of Things, can upgrade the proficiency and adequacy of in an upward direction coordinated tasks. These advances give phenomenal bits of knowledge into creation processes, shopper conduct, and market patterns, empowering associations to go with informed choices and improve their incorporated designs.

The computerized change additionally works with the reconciliation of data across various phases of the store network. Constant information dividing and correspondence among different parts of the incorporated construction upgrade coordination and responsiveness. This interconnectedness smoothes out tasks as well as empowers associations to adjust quickly to changes sought after, store network interruptions, and other outer variables.

All in all, the essential significance of vertical combination is a diverse idea that reaches out past simple functional effectiveness. It includes cost control, inventory network flexibility, quality affirmation, development, separation, and evaluating techniques. Fruitful vertical combination requires a fragile harmony among control and adaptability, as well as a nuanced comprehension of the intricacies related with overseeing different tasks.

While challenges exist, the competitive edges of vertical coordination position it as an important methodology for organizations looking to explore the intricacies of the contemporary business scene. In a period where flexibility and development are principal, the essential significance of vertical joining stays a unique power that shapes the direction of organizations across different businesses. As innovation keeps on advancing, its combination with vertical methodologies enhances the potential for associations to get by as well as flourish in an always changing worldwide commercial center.

6.2. Scalability as a Driver of Tesla's Future Success

As the car business goes through an extraordinary shift towards maintainability and zap, Tesla has arisen as a pioneer, and versatility stands apart as a vital driver of its future achievement. Established by Elon Musk in 2003, Tesla has upset customary thoughts of the car area by delivering electric vehicles (EVs) yet in addition coordinating sustainable power arrangements and progressing independent driving advancements. The outcome of Tesla is complicatedly connected to its capacity to scale its tasks proficiently, develop quickly, and position itself as a forerunner in the worldwide progress to reasonable transportation.

One of the primary components of Tesla's adaptability is its upward coordinated plan of action. Dissimilar to conventional automakers that frequently depend on a perplexing organization of providers for different parts, Tesla produces a huge piece of its parts in-house. This upward reconciliation reaches out from battery creation to electric drivetrain assembling and programming advancement. By controlling basic parts of the store network, Tesla lessens conditions on outer providers, mitigates gambles related with production network interruptions, and oversees creation costs.

The upward incorporation at Tesla is exemplified by its Gigafactories, gigantic creation offices decisively situated all over the planet. These Gigafactories assume a urgent part in the versatility of Tesla's tasks. The Gigafactory idea, started with the development of the Gigafactory 1 in Nevada, addresses a striking move to concentrate and enhance the creation of batteries and drivetrains at a phenomenal scale. The economies of scale accomplished through these Gigafactories contribute fundamentally to cost decrease, making Tesla's electric vehicles more open to a more extensive customer base.

Adaptability, with regards to Tesla, isn't bound to assembling processes alone. The organization's way to deal with programming and man-made brainpower is similarly vital to its versatility system. Tesla vehicles are furnished with cutting edge driver-help frameworks and, now and again, full self-driving capacities. The persistent improvement and organization of these highlights are worked with by over-the-air programming refreshes. This powerful refreshing capacity permits Tesla to upgrade vehicle execution, present new elements, and address wellbeing worries without requiring actual reviews or visits to support focuses. The versatility of Tesla's product driven approach empowers quick development and guarantees that all Tesla vehicles benefit from the most recent headways, making a positive criticism circle for consumer loyalty and brand steadfastness.

Moreover, Tesla's adaptability is apparent in its capacity to grow its product offering. While the organization began with very good quality electric games vehicles, it decisively moved into more standard business sectors with vehicles like the Model S, Model 3, Model X, and Model Y. Each new model addresses a conscious step towards catching a more extensive fragment of the car market. The presentation of the more reasonable Model 3, specifically, denoted a huge achievement as Tesla continued looking for versatility, making electric vehicles more open to a mass market and driving the organization's worldwide deals.

Tesla's introduction to energy arrangements is one more component of its adaptability technique. The organization's procurement of SolarCity in 2016 was a crucial move that lined up with Elon Musk's vision of making a coordinated manageable energy biological system. Through sunlight based chargers, sun oriented rooftop tiles, and energy stockpiling arrangements like the Powerwall and Powerpack, Tesla plans to address the transportation area as well as the more extensive test of progressing to sustainable power.

The versatility of Tesla's energy items is highlighted by its aggressive tasks like the Hornsdale Power Hold in South Australia, an enormous battery stockpiling framework that has exhibited the capability of energy stockpiling to settle power lattices and improve network flexibility.

Tesla's way to deal with adaptability is innately connected to its central goal to speed up the world's progress to supportable energy. The versatility of its electric vehicles and energy arrangements is instrumental in accomplishing this mission at a worldwide scale. The organization's venture into global business sectors, with Gigafactories in China and Germany, further highlights its obligation to making economical transportation and energy arrangements open to assorted populaces. The versatility of Tesla's tasks positions it as a critical player in mature car markets as well as in developing business sectors where the interest for electric vehicles is on the ascent.

In the domain of electric vehicles, the versatility of Tesla's battery innovation is a characterizing factor. The turn of events and creation of elite execution batteries, especially using lithium-particle innovation, have been key to Tesla's prosperity. The organization's attention on further developing energy thickness, decreasing expenses, and expanding creation volumes has been tenacious. The presentation of the 4680 battery cell, a bigger and more energy-thick cell, is a demonstration of Tesla's obligation to pushing the limits of battery innovation. The adaptability of this new battery configuration is supposed to improve the presentation of Tesla vehicles as well as drive down the expense of battery creation, making electric vehicles more reasonable and speeding up the reception bend.

The interconnected idea of Tesla's versatility turns out to be more clear while considering the Supercharger organization. Tesla has put vigorously in building a worldwide organization of quick charging stations, making really long travel and charging helpful for Tesla vehicle proprietors. The versatility of the Supercharger network is an upper hand, making a consistent encounter for Tesla clients and tending to one of the key worries related with electric vehicles — range uneasiness. The proceeded with extension of the Supercharger network lines up with Tesla's obligation to giving dependable foundation that upholds the far reaching reception of electric vehicles.

While the versatility of Tesla's tasks is a foundation of its prosperity, difficulties and reactions exist. One remarkable test is the reliance on key unrefined components for battery creation, like lithium, cobalt, and nickel. The worldwide store network for these materials is dependent upon international and moral worries, and vacillations in costs can affect creation costs. Tesla's capacity to get a steady and maintainable stock of these materials is significant for the drawn out versatility of its battery creation.

Also, the versatility of Tesla's assembling processes has confronted investigation, especially during times of quick development. Creation difficulties, bottlenecks, and deferrals have been accounted for at different places in the organization's set of experiences. Finding some kind of harmony between aggressive creation targets and keeping up with quality guidelines is a persistent test that Tesla faces. The organization's capacity to address these assembling difficulties is critical for supporting its adaptability and satisfying the developing need for its items.

In the more extensive setting of the auto business, the adaptability of electric vehicles is entwined with the improvement of charging foundation and the general shift towards supportable portability. States, industry partners, and buyers assume vital parts in forming the versatility of electric vehicles. Administrative help, motivating forces, and interests in charging foundation are fundamental parts that work with the broad reception of electric vehicles, consequently affecting the adaptability of organizations like Tesla.

Looking forward, the versatility of Tesla's tasks will probably be a definitive figure forming its future achievement. As the organization keeps on extending its product offering, enter new business sectors, and enhance in both equipment and programming, the capacity to scale proficiently and really will be principal. The expected finishing and activity of Gigafactories in Texas and Berlin, as well as the proceeded with development of battery innovation, are demonstrative of Tesla's obligation to versatility. These essential moves position Tesla not just as a market chief in electric vehicles yet in addition as an impetus for the more extensive change of the car business.

All in all, the essential significance of versatility is profoundly imbued in Tesla's DNA and plays had a vital impact in its prosperity. The organization's upward coordinated plan of action, Gigafactories, programming driven approach, item enhancement, and spotlight on feasible energy arrangements on the whole add to its adaptability methodology. As Tesla explores the intricate scene of the car and energy ventures, its obligation to versatility positions it at the very front of the worldwide change to maintainable transportation and energy. The tale of Tesla isn't just one of electric vehicles however a story of versatility, development, and a tenacious quest for a future where practical energy and transportation are the standard instead of the special case.

In the quickly developing scene of the car business, Tesla has arisen as a spearheading force, disturbing customary standards and rethinking the potential outcomes of electric vehicles. At the center of Tesla's future achievement lies a central standard: versatility. The capacity to scale tasks, creation, and mechanical developments has situated Tesla as a leader in the race towards practical transportation.

One of the critical features of adaptability inside Tesla's system is its determined spotlight on propelling battery innovation. Batteries comprise the core of electric vehicles, impacting variables like reach, execution, and by and large effectiveness. Tesla's obligation to adaptability is obvious in its Gigafactories, enormous assembling plants decisively situated across the globe. These offices produce batteries at an exceptional scale as well as address a urgent component in Tesla's methodology to address the developing interest for electric vehicles.

The Gigafactories, considered as a urgent part of Tesla's versatility vision, epitomize the organization's obligation to large scale manufacturing. The Gigafactory in Nevada, frequently alluded to as Gigafactory 1, is a demonstration of Tesla's aggressive scale-up plans. With an impression surpassing 5.3 million square feet, Gigafactory 1 is a rambling complex intended to deliver batteries, battery packs, and powertrains at a remarkable scale. This assembling behemoth makes light of a urgent job in driving the expense of batteries through economies of scale, a vital consider making electric vehicles more open to a more extensive shopper base.

Tesla's Gigafactories stretch out past Nevada, with offices in Shanghai, Berlin, and Texas, each decisively situated to take special care of provincial requests. The Shanghai Gigafactory, for example, upgrades Tesla's creation capacities as well as lines up with the organization's vision to lay out a more grounded presence in the quickly growing Asian market. By decentralizing creation and decisively finding Gigafactories, Tesla guarantees a deft reaction to provincial requests, consequently upgrading its world-wide versatility.

Past actual framework, Tesla's obligation to versatility is profoundly implanted in its product and innovation engineering. The over-the-air (OTA) update capacity, a component coordinated into Tesla vehicles, highlights the organization's spryness in conveying programming improvements at scale. This remote update ability permits Tesla to ceaselessly further develop vehicle execution, present new highlights, and address security worries without requiring actual intercessions. Such versatility in programming organization improves consumer loyalty as well as positions Tesla at the front of advancement in the auto area.

Independent driving innovation is another domain where versatility assumes a urgent part in Tesla's future achievement. Tesla's Autopilot and Full Self-Driving (FSD) capacities are steadily developing, filled by a huge organization of vehicles gathering certifiable information. The versatility of Tesla's independent driving innovation is established in the aggregate knowledge got from the large numbers of vehicles out and about, each adding to the refinement of calculations and the improvement of generally speaking framework execution. The versatility of Tesla's independent driving desires isn't just innovative yet additionally financial, with the possibility to change transportation frameworks on a worldwide scale.

Moreover, Tesla's essential introduction to energy-related adventures enhances the significance of versatility. The Powerwall, Powerpack, and Megapack energy capacity arrangements take special care of private, business, and utility-scale needs, individually.

The versatility of these energy stockpiling arrangements positions Tesla as a central member in the change towards environmentally friendly power. The capacity to convey versatile energy stockpiling arrangements at different levels of the lattice adds to framework soundness, works with the combination of environmentally friendly power sources, and lines up with the more extensive objective of accomplishing a maintainable energy biological system.

Versatility isn't simply bound to creation and innovation for Tesla; it pervades the actual ethos of the organization. The Supercharger organization, Tesla's exclusive quick charging foundation, is an epitome of adaptability in tending to the charging needs of a steadily growing armada of electric vehicles. With Supercharger stations decisively positioned along significant travel courses, Tesla guarantees the versatility of its charging framework to help really long travel, a basic consider advancing the boundless reception of electric vehicles.

Tesla's way to deal with versatility isn't without challenges. The complexities of increasing creation, guaranteeing store network strength, and dealing with the intricacies of a worldwide effort request a degree of hierarchical mastery that couple of organizations have. Tesla's capacity to explore these difficulties, in any case, has been a demonstration of its obligation to versatility as a driver of future achievement.

Additionally, Tesla's vision stretches out past the auto area. The organization's entrance into the private sun powered and energy market further highlights its obligation to adaptable, reasonable arrangements. The Sun based Rooftop, an item that consistently coordinates sun powered innovation with roofing materials, represents Tesla's way to deal with versatility in the sustainable power space. By tending to the private market at scale, Tesla expects to speed up the reception of sun based energy and add to the decentralization of force age.

As Tesla keeps on pushing the limits of development, versatility stays a core value in its quest for reasonable transportation and energy arrangements. The versatility of creation, innovation, and framework not just positions Tesla as an innovator in the electric vehicle market yet in addition lays out an establishment for the organization's venture into different spaces. The essential arrangement of versatility with Tesla's general mission to speed up the world's change to maintainable energy mirrors an all encompassing way to deal with tending to the difficulties representing things to come.

Tesla's progress before very long relies on its capacity to explore the powerful scene of the car and energy enterprises. The organization's obligation to versatility gives a guide to defeating obstructions and quickly jumping all over chances on a worldwide scale. The continuous improvement of new Gigafactories, headways in battery innovation, and the development of independent driving capacities all point towards a future where Tesla's impact reaches out a long ways past the limits of the car area.

All in all, versatility remains as a characterizing mainstay of Tesla's future achievement. From the tremendous Gigafactories creating batteries and vehicles at an extraordinary scale to the organization of over-the-air programming refreshes improving vehicle abilities, Tesla's obligation to adaptability penetrates each part of its activity. As the auto and energy businesses go through extraordinary movements, Tesla's accentuation on versatility positions it as a market chief as well as an impetus for change on a worldwide scale. The versatile idea of Tesla's answers tends to introduce difficulties as well as lays the basis for an economical and versatile future, where electric vehicles and environmentally friendly power assume crucial parts in molding the world's transportation and energy scenes.

Chapter 7

Musk's Influence Beyond Tesla

Elon Musk, a name inseparable from development, disturbance, and vast desire, has risen above the regular limits of business venture to turn into a groundbreaking power in numerous enterprises. While Musk is broadly perceived as the main thrust behind Tesla, his impact reaches out a long ways past electric vehicles. This paper investigates Musk's effect on different areas, digging into the domains of room investigation, sustainable power, transportation, and computerized reasoning.

Tesla, without a doubt, is the crown gem of Musk's enterprising undertakings. Established in 2003, the organization has re-imagined the car business as well as led the worldwide shift towards economical transportation. Musk's vision for Tesla goes past assembling electric vehicles; it incorporates an all encompassing way to deal with energy, including sun based power age, energy capacity arrangements, and the improvement of a thorough charging foundation.

The Tesla Roadster, the organization's debut item, established the groundwork for Musk's desire to speed up the world's change to supportable energy. As the principal interstate lawful electric vehicle with a reach surpassing 200 miles on a solitary charge, the Roadster broke assumptions about the impediments of electric vehicles. Musk's steady faith in the capability of electric impetus, combined with progressions in battery innovation, situated Tesla as an industry pioneer.

Under Musk's initiative, Tesla's impact extended with the presentation of the Model S, an extravagance vehicle that consolidated elite exhibition with a noteworthy reach. The Model S exhibited the practicality of electric vehicles as well as set new norms for advancement in the auto area. Musk's way to deal with mixing state of the art innovation with smooth plan has been a sign of Tesla's prosperity, drawing in a devoted fan base and provoking conventional automakers to reconsider their systems.

In any case, Musk's effect reaches out past the auto scene. SpaceX, established by Musk in 2002, is a demonstration of his daring vision for the fate of room investigation. Musk's objective with SpaceX is to make humankind a multi-planetary animal types, with the possible colonization of Mars as a point of convergence. SpaceX has accomplished striking achievements, including the advancement of the Hawk and Starship rockets, the first secretly supported shuttle to moor with the Worldwide Space Station (ISS), and the continuous organization of the Starlink satellite heavenly body to give worldwide broadband web inclusion.

SpaceX's accomplishments under Musk's administration have upset the avionic business, testing laid out players and presenting uncommon expense efficiencies. The reusable rocket innovation spearheaded by SpaceX has decisively diminished the expense of sending off payloads into space, introducing another time of availability for space investigation. Musk's determined quest for interplanetary colonization mirrors a promise to the drawn out endurance of mankind and an eagerness to handle difficulties considered unrealistic by others.

Musk's impact in the domain of sustainable power is likewise discernible through his contribution with SolarCity, a sun oriented energy administrations organization established by his cousins. Musk assumed a crucial part in the consolidation of Tesla and SolarCity in 2016, shaping a coordinated clean energy organization that offers a thorough set-up of items, from sunlight based chargers and sun oriented rooftop tiles to energy capacity arrangements like the Powerwall and Powerpack.

The SolarCity securing hardened Musk's obligation to tending to the energy change at the two closures: transportation and power age. By joining electric vehicles with sun oriented power and energy stockpiling, Musk imagines a future where people and organizations can meet their energy needs reasonably, liberated from dependence on conventional petroleum derivatives. This all encompassing methodology lines up with Musk's general mission to battle environmental change and lessen humankind's carbon impression.

In the transportation area, Musk's impact stretches out to the improvement of the Hyperloop, a fast transportation framework intended to upset intercity travel. First proposed by Musk in 2013, the Hyperloop imagines traveler units going through low-pressure tubes at close supersonic velocities, lessening travel times between significant urban communities. While the Hyperloop is still in the trial organizes, Musk's vision for a quicker, more productive method of transportation mirrors his penchant for testing traditional standards.

Musk's commitment with transportation isn't bound to Earth. The Exhausting Organization, one more endeavor initiated by Musk, means to address metropolitan clog through the development of underground transportation burrows. The idea, known as the Circle, imagines an organization of passages where independent electric vehicles transport travelers at high paces. By going underground, Musk intends to ease superficial traffic, giving a versatile answer for metropolitan transportation challenges.

Man-made reasoning (artificial intelligence) is another field where Musk has made critical commitments and communicated remarkable worries. OpenAI, a man-made intelligence research lab established by Musk and others, centers around creating counterfeit general knowledge (AGI) while guaranteeing its dependable and safe organization. Musk's support for moral simulated intelligence rehearses and the requirement for administrative oversight mirrors his attention to the potential dangers related with cutting edge computer based intelligence frameworks.

Regardless of his commitments to man-made intelligence improvement, Musk has been vocal about the likely risks of uncontrolled artificial intelligence, cautioning against the production of hyper-savvy frameworks that could present existential dangers to humankind. His interests have filled conversations about the moral ramifications of simulated intelligence and the need for proactive measures to guarantee the mindful improvement of man-made brainpower innovations.

Musk's impact isn't simply restricted to the organizations he established however reaches out to businesses he has entered. His public persona and commitment via online entertainment stages have made him a polarizing figure, with a huge following and an equivalent portion of pundits. Musk's tweets, frequently unfiltered and capricious, have the ability to influence monetary business sectors, impact general assessment, and even effect the stock costs of his own organizations.

The erraticisms of Musk's character have become fundamental to his public picture, adding a layer of flightiness to his undertakings. Whether declaring aggressive courses of events for item delivers, participating in talk via web-based entertainment, or exhibiting a style for the emotional during item unveilings, Musk's way to deal with correspondence has separate him from conventional Chiefs. While this unconventional style has earned both recognition and analysis, it obviously adds to the religion like following encompassing Musk and his endeavors.

Musk's impact likewise reaches out to the electric vehicle market at large. The outcome of Tesla has prodded laid out automakers to speed up their electric vehicle plans, put resources into battery innovation, and redo their item portfolios. Musk's vision for an electric future has catalyzed a change in outlook in the auto business, provoking contenders to reconsider their systems and focus on reasonable transportation arrangements.

Besides, Musk's effect on the monetary business sectors has been significant. The ascent of Tesla's stock cost, frequently determined by Musk's tweets and item declarations, has made Tesla perhaps of the most significant automaker on the planet. Musk's capacity to spellbind financial backers and fuel market excitement has situated him as a focal figure in conversations about the crossing point of innovation, money, and development.

While Musk's impact is evident, it isn't without debate. His administration style at Tesla has confronted investigation, with reports of extraordinary workplaces, high worker turnover, and work questions. Musk's public assertions, particularly via virtual entertainment, have prompted lawful difficulties and administrative examinations. The unconventionalities that add to his public persona have likewise ignited banters about the moral obligations of compelling figures in the business world.

Taking everything into account, Elon Musk's impact reaches out a long ways past the bounds of Tesla. From altering the auto business with electric vehicles to rethinking space investigation with SpaceX, Musk's effect traverses numerous areas. His introductions to environmentally friendly power, transportation, man-made brainpower, and passage development mirror a visionary way to deal with tackling complex difficulties. Musk's capacity to motivate, upset, and lead has made a permanent imprint on the business world, molding the direction of enterprises and affecting the worldwide discussion on innovation and advancement. As Musk keeps on pushing the limits of what is considered potential, his impact is probably going to reverberate across different areas, leaving a persevering through heritage in the chronicles of business venture and mechanical headway.

7.1. Impact on Industry Dynamics and Consumer Behavior

Elon Musk's endeavors, especially Tesla and SpaceX, have reshaped whole businesses as well as significantly affected industry elements and buyer conduct. From the car area to space investigation, Musk's creative methodologies have constrained customary players to reexamine their techniques, embrace supportability, and adjust to changing customer assumptions. This article digs into the groundbreaking impact Musk's endeavors have had on industry elements and how they have in a general sense changed customer conduct.

Auto Area Change:

Tesla's Ascent and Industry Reaction:

Tesla's climb in the car business has been downright progressive. Musk's vision for electric vehicles (EVs) tested the ordinary idea that reasonable driving implied thinking twice about execution and style. The progress of Tesla's Model S and resulting models has constrained laid out automakers to speed up their electric vehicle plans. Musk's faithful obligation to pushing the limits of battery innovation has made EVs more open as well as set another norm for reach, execution, and development.

Shift Towards Electric Portability:

Musk's effect stretches out past Tesla, catalyzing a more extensive shift towards electric versatility. Heritage automakers, at first reluctant to put resources into EVs, have begun committing huge assets to charge. Musk's vision has sped up the advancement of electric vehicle environments, affecting charging foundation extension and cultivating associations among automakers and innovation organizations. The car area, when overwhelmed by gas powered motors, is currently encountering a change in perspective driven by Musk's steady quest for manageable transportation.

Customer Assumptions and Inclinations:

Tesla's prosperity has re-imagined customer assumptions in the auto area. Musk's accentuation on state of the art innovation, over-the-air programming refreshes, and independent driving capacities has made another benchmark for what customers expect in a cutting edge vehicle. The interest for electric vehicles has flooded, and shoppers presently focus on supportability, mechanical advancement, and ecological effect while pursuing buying choices. Musk's impact has changed the story around electric vehicles from specialty options in contrast to standard, optimistic decisions.

Space Investigation and Airplane business Disturbance:
SpaceX's Reshaping of Aviation Standards:

In the airplane business, Musk's SpaceX has upset customary standards and tested laid out players. The coming of reusable rocket innovation, spearheaded by SpaceX, has emphatically decreased the expense of room travel. Musk's vision of making space investigation more reasonable and available has not just opened up open doors for business satellite send-offs yet has additionally reignited the chance of human investigation past Earth. SpaceX's accomplishments, for example, the first secretly subsidized space apparatus to dock with the Global Space Station (ISS), highlight Musk's obligation to changing the aviation scene.

Serious Scene and Commercialization of Room:

SpaceX's prosperity has provoked different organizations to reconsider their techniques and put resources into reusable rocket innovation. Musk's effect reaches out past SpaceX's own undertakings, impacting the cutthroat scene of the aeronautic trade. The commercialization of room, once overwhelmed by government organizations, has seen a flood in confidential area contribution. Musk's endeavors have shown the way that space investigation can be a reasonable and productive business, prodding another time of business in the aviation area.

Moving Another Age:

Musk's undertakings in space investigation have caught the creative mind of another age. The possibility of colonizing Mars and the daring vision of making mankind a multi-planetary animal varieties have enlivened youthful personalities to seek after vocations in science, innovation, designing, and math (STEM).

Musk's impact goes past industry elements; it has turned into an impetus for encouraging logical interest and investigation, molding the desires of people in the future.

Environmentally friendly power and Feasible Arrangements:
SolarCity and Combination with Tesla:

Musk's impact stretches out to the sustainable power area through his contribution with SolarCity. The combination of SolarCity into Tesla's portfolio denoted an essential move to make a thorough clean energy organization. Musk's vision for a reasonable future envelops electric vehicles as well as sun oriented power age, energy capacity, and a versatile answer for a completely incorporated clean energy environment.

Influence on Energy Framework:

Tesla's Powerwall, Powerpack, and Megapack energy capacity arrangements, joined with sun oriented innovation, can possibly reshape energy foundation. Musk's emphasis on versatility in energy arrangements positions Tesla as a central participant in tending to framework security, supporting the coordination of environmentally friendly power sources, and decentralizing power age. The effect reaches out past individual customers to impact how networks and areas approach energy manageability.

Difficulties to Customary Utilities:

The ascent of Tesla's energy arrangements presents difficulties to conventional utility models. Musk's vision for decentralized energy age and capacity upsets the traditional worldview of incorporated power plants. This change in energy elements provokes laid out utilities to adjust, put resources into sustainable power sources, and embrace the versatility of circulated energy arrangements. Musk's impact in this area highlights the interconnectedness of transportation and energy and their aggregate effect on supportability.

Transportation Developments:

Hyperloop and Metropolitan Transportation:

Musk's effect on industry elements reaches out to transportation advancements past electric vehicles. The idea of the Hyperloop, a high velocity transportation framework, provokes customary ways to deal with intercity travel. Musk's vision for the Hyperloop mirrors a promise to changing metropolitan transportation, diminishing travel times, and tending to blockage. While the Hyperloop is still in the exploratory stages, Musk's impact has prodded conversations and interests in elective methods of transportation.

The Wearing Organization's Underground Transportation out:

The Exhausting Organization, one more endeavor drove by Musk, plans to address metropolitan clog through the development of underground transportation burrows. The Circle idea imagines an organization of passages where independent electric vehicles transport travelers at high rates.

Musk's way to deal with addressing metropolitan transportation challenges features the requirement for versatile arrangements that can adjust to the developing requests of urbanization.

Purchaser Reception of New Transportation Ideal models:

Musk's endeavors in transportation developments can possibly reshape how individuals move inside urban communities and between metropolitan focuses. While these ideas are still in beginning phases, their effect on industry elements and conversations around the eventual fate of transportation is obvious. Musk's capacity to present flighty thoughts and gather public interest has started discussions about the requirement for inventive answers for address the intricacies of current transportation.

Impact on Purchaser Conduct:

Moving Inclinations Towards Supportability:

Musk's endeavors play had a crucial impact in molding shopper conduct, especially in the car area. The progress of Tesla has shown the way that maintainability and execution can coincide, testing the discernment that electric vehicles think twice about driving experience. Customers, enlivened by Musk's vision, are progressively focusing on maintainability in their buying choices, affecting different businesses to embrace naturally cognizant practices.

Assumptions for Mechanical Advancement:

Buyers presently expect constant mechanical advancement in the items they buy. Musk's accentuation on over-the-air programming refreshes, independent driving capacities, and state of the art innovation has set another norm for purchaser assumptions. This shift goes past the car area, impacting how customers see mechanical progressions and requesting a steady development of items to measure up to these assumptions.

Influence on Brand Reliability:

Musk's public persona and capricious correspondence style add to mark unwaveringness for Tesla and his different endeavors. Buyers are attracted not exclusively to the items yet additionally to Musk's visionary authority and strong articulations. The religion like following encompassing Musk has made an exceptional dynamic where shopper unwaveringness stretches out past conventional brand loyalties, underlining the impact of individual characters in molding customer conduct.

Moving Business and Development:

Musk's pioneering venture and the progress of his endeavors have roused another flood of business and development. Business visionaries in different ventures are persuaded by Musk's capacity to challenge standards, take on bold objectives, and disturb laid out areas. This impact reaches out to shopper conduct as people progressively look for items and administrations that line up with a feeling of development and maintainability.

Difficulties and Discussions:

Work environment Elements and Work Practices:

Musk's administration style, described by extraordinary workplaces and exclusive standards, has confronted examination. Reports of work environment challenges at Tesla, including high representative turnover and work debates, bring up issues about the harmony among development and worker prosperity. The effect on industry elements remembers expanded consideration for work environment rehearses, with conversations around the moral obligations of pioneers in cultivating sound workplaces.

Administrative Investigation and Lawful Difficulties:

Musk's public assertions, especially via web-based entertainment, have prompted lawful difficulties and administrative examination. From SEC examinations to legitimate disagreements regarding business choices and public correspondence, Musk's endeavors have explored a complex lawful scene. This examination has suggestions for industry elements as controllers survey the requirement for oversight and responsibility in areas impacted by Musk's endeavors.

Moral Contemplations in Man-made brainpower:

Musk's contribution in OpenAI mirrors his consciousness of the moral contemplations related with computerized reasoning. The discussion over the mindful turn of events and organization of computer based intelligence innovations is a critical part of Musk's effect on industry elements. The effect reaches out to conversations about the moral ramifications of cutting edge computer based intelligence frameworks and the requirement for administrative oversight to guarantee the capable utilization of man-made brainpower.

Elon Musk's effect on industry elements and purchaser conduct is multi-layered and broad. From changing the car area with Tesla's electric vehicles to reshaping space investigation through SpaceX, Musk's endeavors have disturbed customary businesses as well as impacted more extensive discussions about supportability, development, and the fate of innovation. As shoppers progressively focus on supportability and mechanical advancement, Musk's impact is probably going to persevere, proceeding to shape the direction of ventures and customer assumptions in the years to come.

7.2. Shaping Global Perspectives on Sustainable Transportation

Elon Musk's visionary interests in feasible transportation, basically through Tesla, have altogether molded worldwide viewpoints on the practicality and attractiveness of electric vehicles (EVs). Past only acquainting electric vehicles with the market, Musk plays had a groundbreaking impact in modifying the story around supportable transportation, affecting purchaser perspectives, provoking expansive moves, and cultivating a more extensive cultural hug of clean energy options.

Tesla's Spearheading Job:

At the core of Musk's effect is Tesla's spearheading job in making electric vehicles both optimistic and available. The presentation of the Tesla Roadster in 2008 denoted an essential defining moment, showing the way that electric vehicles could be elite execution, mechanically progressed, and tastefully engaging. Musk's accentuation on consolidating manageability with extravagance and execution tested winning generalizations about electric vehicles as utilitarian or thinking twice about driving experience.

Purchaser Discernment and Reception:

Musk's impact on worldwide viewpoints starts with adjusting shopper impression of electric vehicles. Generally saw as specialty or unfeasible, EVs acquired another standing under Musk's direction. The progress of Tesla's Model S, Model 3, and different models displayed that electric vehicles could coordinate or surpass their inward burning partners concerning reach, speed increase, and generally driving experience. Thus, shopper mentalities moved from doubt to expectation, with electric vehicles turning into an image of development and natural obligation.

Advocating Manageability:

Musk's obligation to maintainability reaches out past the actual vehicles. The combination of sunlight based energy arrangements into Tesla's portfolio, exemplified by the procurement of SolarCity, mirrors an all encompassing way to deal with tending to ecological worries. Musk's vision for an economical future incorporates zero-emanation vehicles as well as a thorough environment where sustainable power age and capacity assume crucial parts. This coordinated methodology lines up with worldwide endeavors to battle environmental change and decrease reliance on petroleum derivatives.

Worldwide Effect on Automakers:

The effect of Musk's vision on worldwide viewpoints stretches out to customary automakers. At first pretentious of electric vehicles, many laid out automakers recalibrated their procedures because of Tesla's prosperity. Musk's accentuation on execution, development, and a promise to consistent improvement constrained contenders to speed up their electric vehicle programs, put resources into battery innovation, and reposition their brands in arrangement with changing shopper inclinations.

Speeding up the Shift to Electric:

Musk's impact in forming worldwide points of view on manageable transportation is confirmed by the speed increase of the shift to electric vehicles across the auto business. States overall are carrying out strategies to energize EV reception, from impetuses for customers to rigid emanation guidelines for producers. Musk's promotion for maintainable practices has added to the more extensive acknowledgment of electric vehicles as a feasible and essential part representing things to come of transportation.

Difficulties to The norm:

The interruption brought about by Musk's vision reaches out past the auto area. Customary service stations, long the foundation of refueling framework, face difficulties as electric vehicles become more common. Musk's accentuation on a Supercharger organization, an exclusive quick charging framework for Tesla vehicles, has prodded conversations about the requirement for a complete and versatile charging foundation to help the developing armada of electric vehicles. This test to business as usual highlights the groundbreaking effect of Musk's reasonable transportation vision on laid out industry standards.

Worldwide Development and Territorial Transformation:

Tesla's worldwide development under Musk's initiative has been a urgent calculate forming worldwide points of view on reasonable transportation. Gigafactories decisively situated in various regions of the planet, from Nevada and Shanghai to Berlin and Texas, mean a promise to versatile creation as well as an affirmation of the significance of provincial variation. Musk's methodology perceives the extraordinary difficulties and open doors in different business sectors, taking special care of provincial requests and encouraging a more boundless acknowledgment of electric vehicles worldwide.

Advancements Past Electric Vehicles:

Musk's impact on worldwide points of view reaches out past electric vehicles to include a more extensive vision for the fate of transportation. The Hyperloop, a rapid transportation framework, and The Exhausting Organization's underground transportation burrows address creative answers for address metropolitan clog and reclassify the boundaries of proficient travel. These endeavors, while in different progressive phases, add to forming worldwide points of view on what is conceivable in the domain of maintainable and proficient transportation.

Electric Vehicles as Mechanical Stages:

Musk's impact stretches out to conceptualizing electric vehicles as methods of transportation as well as innovative stages. The over-the-air programming refreshes, a sign of Tesla vehicles, epitomize Musk's obligation to nonstop improvement and development. Conventional vehicles go through steady changes during yearly model updates, while Tesla vehicles can get critical element upgrades and execution enhancements from a distance. This approach difficulties the conventional lifecycle of autos and stresses the significance of programming in the advancement of transportation.

The Job of Musk's Persona:

Musk's own image and public persona assume a huge part in forming worldwide points of view on maintainable transportation. His perceivability via web-based entertainment, unfiltered correspondence style, and direct commitment with general society add to an exceptional story encompassing Tesla and Musk himself.

The blend of his pioneering achievement, aggressive objectives, and straightforward methodology has transformed Musk into an image of development, pushing the limits of what is conceivable and testing the customary way of thinking.

Media Impact and Market Feeling:

Musk's presence via web-based entertainment stages, especially Twitter, has turned into an incredible asset impacting market feeling and molding worldwide viewpoints. Musk's tweets, declarations, and connections with people in general can prompt critical vacillations in Tesla's stock cost and effect the more extensive electric vehicle market. This powerful connection among Musk and the media adds to a persistent exchange about Tesla, supportable transportation, and the eventual fate of the auto business.

Difficulties and Reactions:

While Musk's impact has been extraordinary, it has not been without difficulties and reactions. The extreme examination of Tesla's Autopilot framework, worries about work environment rehearses, and lawful issues connected with Musk's correspondence via virtual entertainment highlight the intricacies of driving an organization that is at the front of significantly impacting worldwide points of view on transportation. Musk's unfiltered correspondence style, while adding to his public persona, has additionally prompted debates that require cautious administration to explore.

Worldwide Cooperation and Advancement:

Musk's effect on worldwide points of view rises above individual organizations and areas. His receptiveness to imparting Tesla's licenses to different automakers, a move pointed toward encouraging joint effort and speeding up the shift to manageable transportation, shows an acknowledgment of the aggregate test of battling environmental change. Musk's impact stretches out to empowering worldwide coordinated effort and advancement to address normal difficulties connected with transportation, discharges, and natural supportability.

Instructive and Motivational Effect:

Musk's impact stretches out past his nearby undertakings to instructive and persuasive domains. His undertakings with SpaceX and the vision of colonizing Mars have caught the creative mind of individuals around the world. The possibility of humankind turning into a multi-planetary animal groups under Musk's vision motivates a feeling of marvel and interest, particularly among more youthful ages. Musk's effect on worldwide viewpoints isn't just about unmistakable items yet additionally about forming a story that empowers investigation, development, and a promise to supportability.

Elon Musk's effect on forming worldwide viewpoints on feasible transportation is diverse, going from changing purchaser perspectives and industry elements to cultivating a more extensive cultural hug of clean energy choices.

Through Tesla and different endeavors, Musk has not just made electric vehicles a pragmatic and beneficial decision yet has likewise catalyzed a change in how the perspectives transportation. The continuous impact of Musk's vision is probably going to reach out far into the future, proceeding to move advancement, challenge laid out standards, and add to the continuous worldwide discourse about the crossing point of innovation, supportability, and the fate of transportation.

Elon Musk, through his leading undertakings, has transformed into an unprecedented power in shaping overall perspectives on sensible transportation. At the actual front of this advancement is Tesla, the electric vehicle (EV) association laid out by Musk in 2003. Musk's vision goes past essentially creating electric vehicles; it incorporates an exhaustive framework to rename the vehicle business, develop viability, and effect how social orders see and take on innocuous to the environment techniques for transportation. This article examines Musk's impact on overall perspectives concerning efficient transportation and how Tesla's improvements have added to the persistent change in standpoint in the vehicle region.

Tesla's Work in Reconsidering Reasonable Transportation:

Tesla, under Elon Musk's organization, has been instrumental in making waves of the vehicle business. Musk's principal objective to accelerate the world's change to plausible energy is exemplified in Tesla's commitment to electric adaptability. The association's advancement in making electric vehicles that match as well as outflank the show of standard internal combustion engine vehicles has reshaped the record around viability and excess.

One of Tesla's underlying jump advances was the introduction of the Tesla Roadster, the essential turnpike genuine electric vehicle with a basic reach. This model showed the capacity of electric vehicles as well as broken suppositions about their limitations with respect to speed, reach, and execution. Musk's framework with the Roadster was imperative; by starting with a first in class sports vehicle, he showed that electric vehicles could be indistinguishable from luxury and tip top execution, testing the wisdom that they were only sensible for short drives.

Mass Market Charm:

Tesla's impact on overall perspectives connects past the excess part with the introduction of the Model S, Model 3, Model X, and Model Y. Musk's accentuation on conveying electric vehicles to the mass market has been a particular benefit. The Model S, an excess vehicle, merged tip top execution with a vital reach, making electric vehicles charming to a greater group. The following appearance of the more sensible Model 3 further solidified Tesla's circumstance as a precursor in the EV market, moving customary automakers to work with their electric vehicle plans.

Improvements in Battery Development:

Imperative to Tesla's result in affordable transportation is its consistent mission for degrees of progress in battery advancement. The association's Gigafactories, conclusively arranged across the globe, are an exhibition of Musk's commitment to flexibility and the enormous scope assembling of batteries.

The economies of scale achieved through these Gigafactories add to driving down the cost of batteries, an essential consider making electric vehicles more open to a greater client base.

Musk's forceful plans for Gigafactories connect past electric vehicles. These workplaces are important to Tesla's vision of making a down to earth energy natural framework. The enormous scope assembling of batteries drives Tesla's electric vehicles as well as supports energy limit deals with any consequences regarding private, business, and utility-scale applications. This association of electric vehicles and energy amassing positions Tesla as a comprehensive game plan provider in the greater setting of viable transportation and energy use.

Charging Establishment and Arrive at Anxiety:

Musk saw every step of the way that for electric vehicles to secure vast gathering, having a tendency to run apprehension and building a strong charging system were essential. Tesla's Supercharger association, a prohibitive speedy charging system, has been a fundamental part in trim overall perspectives on electric vehicle practicality. These Superchargers, conclusively arranged along huge travel courses, outfit Tesla owners with the sureness that truly lengthy travel isn't simply possible anyway worthwhile.

The Supercharger network similarly reflects Musk's historic methodology. By placing assets into a selective charging establishment, Tesla has separate itself from various automakers and arranged itself as an industry boss. Musk's emphasis on system improvement isn't just about supporting Tesla vehicles anyway is a fundamental move to address an essential limit to wide EV gathering generally. As extra automakers enter the electric vehicle market, the prerequisite for a standardized and wide charging establishment ends up being logically clear.

Autonomous Driving Development:

Past the indisputable pieces of electric vehicles and charging system, Musk's effect on overall perspectives connects with the area of autonomous driving advancement. Tesla's Autopilot and Full Self-Driving (FSD) limits address a tremendous step towards a future where vehicles are electric as well as prepared for investigating roads freely. While the improvement of totally free vehicles is at this point a work in progress', areas of strength for Musk has begun conversations and moved perceptions about the possible destiny of transportation.

Tesla's method for managing autonomous driving is amazing in that it utilize the total information got from the enormous quantities of Tesla vehicles making the rounds. Musk's decision to send vehicles with hardware fit for supporting free features, joined with the consistent combination of genuine data, positions Tesla as a forerunner in the race towards totally free vehicles. The consistent types of progress in Tesla's Autopilot structure show Musk's commitment to stretching the boundaries of what is reachable in the space of self-driving advancement.

Overall Environmental Impact and Reasonability:

Musk's impact on overall perspectives as for useful transportation connects with the greater natural impact of electric vehicles. The shift from internal combustion engine vehicles to electric vehicles is seen as a crucial push toward directing the biological impact of transportation. Musk's help for reasonability lines up with creating overall stresses over ecological change and air quality.

By upholding electric vehicles, Musk has added to changing perceptions about the gig of transportation in regular debasement. Electric vehicles produce zero tailpipe surges, decreasing the overall carbon impression related with individual transportation. As councils and buyers in general become more mindful of natural issues, Musk's vision for a plausible future resounds with an overall group.

Challenges and Responses:

While Musk and Tesla have made immense strides in reshaping overall perspectives on legitimate transportation, there are troubles and responses that ought to be perceived. The biological impact of collecting electric vehicles, particularly the extraction of regular substances for batteries, is a concern. Musk's commitment to legitimacy should wrap the utilitarian time of vehicles as well as the entire life cycle, including creation and end-of-life examinations.

Besides, the receptiveness of electric vehicles to a greater monetary fragment remains a test. While Tesla has gained ground in offering more sensible models, there is still work to be done to ensure that functional transportation isn't limited to those in that frame of mind of pay. Musk's vision for the mass-market appeal of electric vehicles ought to continue to address moderateness and receptiveness to really influence overall transportation components.

Government Procedures and Establishment Improvement:

Musk's effect is moreover complicatedly joined to government systems and sponsorship for efficient transportation. The result of electric vehicles relies upon mechanical types of progress as well as on a consistent regulatory environment. States in general expect a critical part in supporting the gathering of electric vehicles, making charging structure, and progressing doable transportation plans.

Musk's supporting for reasonability integrates dynamic responsibility with policymakers to ensure that regulatory frameworks engage the improvement of the electric vehicle market. Besides, Musk's effect loosens up to discussions about the prerequisite for standardized charging shows, overall composed exertion on legitimacy goals, and the occupation of state run organizations in working with the change to electric movability.

Elon Musk's impact on framing overall perspectives on sensible transportation is different and broad. Through Tesla, Musk has made electric vehicles hopeful as well as laid the reason for a greater difference in the vehicle business.

His vision wraps the genuine vehicles as well as the entire climate, recollecting movements for battery development, charging system, and the blend of feasible power.

As the world grapples with the hardships of ecological change and searches for extra reasonable strategies for transportation, Musk's effect is most likely going to create. The constant headways in battery advancement, the improvement of charging system, and the journey for autonomous abilities to drive are normal for Musk's commitment to stretching the boundaries of what is possible in the space of plausible transportation. While challenges persevere, Musk's vision for a destiny of electric, free, and prudent movability has undoubtedly made a super durable engraving on the overall comprehension, influencing how we drive as well as how we envision the destiny of transportation.

Chapter 8

Conclusion

Taking everything into account, Elon Musk's vision has been the directing power behind Tesla's momentous achievement and its extraordinary effect on the auto business. Musk's bold objective of speeding up the world's progress to maintainable energy isn't simply a grandiose desire yet a key guide that has pushed Tesla into an administrative role in the electric vehicle (EV) market. From upsetting the view of electric vehicles to pushing the limits of innovation, Musk's vision stretches out past the car area, incorporating environmentally friendly power, space investigation, and economical transportation all in all.

At the core of Musk's vision for Tesla is the obligation to maintainability. By making electric vehicles that adversary as well as outperform conventional gas powered motor vehicles in execution, plan, and reach, Musk has moved the worldview of what is conceivable in the auto business. The outcome of Tesla's models, from the notable Roadster to the more open Model 3, mirrors Musk's essential way to deal with make manageable transportation interesting to an expansive buyer base. The mass-market allure of Tesla's vehicles has tested conventional automakers as well as impacted worldwide points of view on the suitability and attractiveness of electric versatility.

Tesla's interest in battery innovation and the foundation of Gigafactories embody Musk's obligation to versatility and large scale manufacturing. The economies of scale accomplished through these offices contribute not exclusively to decreasing the expense of batteries yet in addition to situating Tesla as an exhaustive energy arrangements supplier. The mix of environmentally friendly power sources, energy capacity arrangements, and electric vehicles into a bound together biological system mirrors Musk's comprehensive vision for a feasible energy future. Tesla's energy items, including the Powerwall, Powerpack, and Megapack, highlight Musk's obligation to tending to the transportation area as well as more extensive energy challenges.

Musk's effect on the auto business goes past the substantial parts of vehicle creation. The Supercharger organization, Tesla's exclusive quick charging foundation, addresses a basic hindrance to far reaching electric vehicle reception by reducing range tension and working with really long travel. By putting resources into a restrictive charging foundation, Musk has upheld Tesla proprietors as well as set a norm for the business. The significance of framework advancement, especially as a team with different automakers, is pivotal for the proceeded with development of the electric vehicle market internationally.

The impact of Musk's vision is additionally obvious in Tesla's introduction to independent driving innovation. The arrangement of vehicles with equipment equipped for supporting independent highlights, combined with persistent over-the-air programming refreshes, mirrors Musk's obligation to pushing the limits of what is feasible in self-driving innovation. While the acknowledgment of completely independent vehicles is a continuous excursion, Musk's striking vision has ignited discussions and moved viewpoints about the eventual fate of transportation.

Past the auto area, Musk's impact reaches out to SpaceX, where his vision for the colonization of Mars and the improvement of reusable rocket innovation has disturbed customary standards in the aeronautic trade. SpaceX's accomplishments, including the first secretly subsidized rocket to dock with the Global Space Station and the continuous organization of the Starlink satellite heavenly body, highlight Musk's obligation to making space investigation more reasonable and open. The effect of Musk's vision stretches out past industry elements to move another age of trailblazers and fuel interest in STEM fields.

While Musk's vision has pushed Tesla to phenomenal levels, it isn't without difficulties and reactions. The extraordinary workplaces at Tesla, reports of high representative turnover, and work questions feature the intricacies of offsetting advancement with representative prosperity. Musk's public assertions and offbeat correspondence style have additionally prompted lawful difficulties and administrative investigation. These difficulties, while highlighting the intricacies of authority in a quickly developing industry, have not cheapened the general effect of Musk's vision on the direction of Tesla and the ventures it works in.

Looking forward, Musk's vision will keep on forming Tesla's future achievement. The continuous advancements in battery innovation, the extension of charging framework, and the quest for completely independent driving capacities show that Musk's obligation to pushing the limits of development stays relentless. Tesla's essential drives, including the development of new Gigafactories, passage into new business sectors, and headways in energy-related adventures, line up with Musk's all-encompassing mission of speeding up the world's change to economical energy.

The worldwide viewpoint on feasible transportation, impacted fundamentally by Musk's vision, is going through a significant change. Electric vehicles are not generally seen as a specialty market however as a standard, optimistic decision. Legislatures, enterprises, and customers overall are progressively perceiving the basic of embracing supportable transportation answers for address natural difficulties and diminish reliance on petroleum products. Musk's vision, with its accentuation on mechanical development, versatility, and an all encompassing way to deal with energy arrangements, has situated Tesla at the front of this groundbreaking movement.

All in all, Elon Musk's vision for Tesla epitomizes something beyond the making of electric vehicles; it addresses a change in outlook by they way we see, produce, and use energy for transportation. His brassy objectives, combined with a steady quest for development, have not just pushed Tesla to the very front of the car and energy ventures however have likewise impacted worldwide points of view on manageability and the fate of transportation. As Tesla proceeds to develop and explore the difficulties of the quickly evolving scene, Musk's visionary initiative remaining parts a main thrust, molding the direction of Tesla's future achievement and leaving a persevering through heritage in the chronicles of business and innovation.

8.1. Reflection on Musk's Vision and Tesla's Lasting Legacy

As we consider Elon Musk's vision and Tesla's enduring heritage, it becomes obvious that both are permanently entwined, addressing an extraordinary power that has reclassified ventures, tested standards, and impacted worldwide viewpoints on innovation, maintainability, and development. Musk's vision, described by daringness, versatility, and a pledge to practical energy, has impelled Tesla to remarkable levels as well as made a getting through imprint on the auto, energy, and space investigation areas.

Musk's Vision: An Impetus for Change

At the center of Musk's vision is a constant quest for aggressive objectives that stretch out past the limits of customary reasoning. The overall mission to speed up the world's change to feasible energy fills in as a core value, controlling Tesla towards development and disturbance. Musk's essential premonition is clear in his way to deal with industry challenges, where he distinguishes potential open doors for adaptable arrangements that rise above individual business sectors.

The boldness of Musk's vision is maybe most obvious in Tesla's introduction to the electric vehicle (EV) market. At the point when Musk established Tesla in 2003, the auto scene was overwhelmed by gas powered motors, and efficiently manufactured electric vehicles appeared to be unrealistic. Musk's vision, in any case, saw electric vehicles not as specialty choices but rather as the eventual fate of transportation. His obligation to making EVs standard and optimistic was an intense takeoff according to regular industry viewpoints.

Versatility is a common subject in Musk's vision, clear in the development of Gigafactories intended to efficiently manufacture batteries and electric vehicles. The Gigafactories, decisively situated all over the planet, embody Musk's obligation to driving down costs through economies of scale. This emphasis on versatility isn't restricted to Tesla's car tries yet reaches out to the energy area, where Musk imagines an all encompassing clean energy biological system that coordinates electric vehicles, sunlight based power age, and energy stockpiling arrangements.

Musk's vision is likewise set apart by a steadfast obligation to manageability. The quest for electric versatility isn't just about making superior execution vehicles however about tending to natural difficulties and diminishing mankind's reliance on non-renewable energy sources. Musk's promotion for reasonable energy arrangements lines up with worldwide endeavors to battle environmental change, situating Tesla as a vital participant in the progress to a low-carbon future.

Tesla's Enduring Heritage: Changing Businesses

The tradition of Tesla is entwined with Musk's vision, addressing a change in outlook by they way we see and connect with innovation, energy, and transportation. As we dive into Tesla's effect on different enterprises, obviously its inheritance stretches out past the development of electric vehicles.

Car Industry Change:

At its center, Tesla has re-imagined the auto business. Musk's vision to make electric vehicles standard has disturbed the customary car story, testing laid out players and catalyzing a more extensive shift towards manageable transportation. The outcome of Tesla's vehicles, from the very good quality Roadster to the more available Model 3, has not just exhibited the market allure of electric vehicles yet has additionally set new benchmarks for execution, reach, and innovation.

Tesla's impact is obvious in the speed increase of electric vehicle reception universally. Laid out automakers, at first wary about putting resources into electric portability, are presently scrambling to foster their electric vehicle arrangements. Musk's vision has pushed electric vehicles from a specialty market to a standard decision, impacting customer inclinations and reshaping the serious scene of the auto business.

The tradition of Tesla likewise reaches out to headways in battery innovation. The Gigafactories, with their accentuation on large scale manufacturing, have upheld Tesla's electric vehicle creation as well as added to the improvement of energy stockpiling arrangements. Tesla's Powerwall, Powerpack, and Megapack, controlled by cutting edge battery innovation, have suggestions past individual families — they offer versatile answers for lattice steadiness, environmentally friendly power mix, and the decentralization of force age.

Energy Area Coordination:

Tesla's inheritance isn't bound to electric vehicles; it includes a more extensive vision for a supportable energy biological system. The reconciliation of sun oriented power age, energy capacity, and electric vehicles positions Tesla as a thorough clean energy organization. The procurement of SolarCity, Musk's association in environmentally friendly power, and the advancement of sun based rooftop tiles highlight Tesla's obligation to tending to the energy change from numerous points.

The Powerwall, a home battery framework, permits customers to store overabundance energy created by sunlight based chargers for use during top interest or blackouts. The bigger scope Powerpack and Megapack arrangements are intended for business and utility-scale applications, offering network adjustment, load adjusting, and support for environmentally friendly power reconciliation. Tesla's endeavors in energy arrangements are lined up with Musk's more extensive vision of making an economical and decentralized energy foundation.

The effect of Tesla's energy arrangements isn't restricted to individual customers or organizations; it stretches out to the lattice in general. As sustainable power sources become more predominant, the versatility of Tesla's energy stockpiling arrangements adds to conquering difficulties connected with discontinuity and fluctuation. This coordination of electric vehicles, sun oriented power, and energy stockpiling positions Tesla as a central member in molding the eventual fate of energy utilization and dissemination.

Space Investigation and Aviation Disturbance:

Tesla's inheritance isn't bound to Earth; it reaches out to the domains of room investigation through Musk's other endeavor, SpaceX. While unmistakable from Tesla, SpaceX typifies Musk's vision for pushing the limits of what is conceivable. SpaceX's accomplishments, from the advancement of the Bird of prey and Starship rockets to the arrangement of the Starlink satellite heavenly body, highlight Musk's obligation to making space investigation more available and savvy.

SpaceX's reusable rocket innovation, spearheaded under Musk's administration, has disturbed the airplane business. The capacity to recuperate and reuse rocket parts has decisively decreased the expense of room travel, testing the conventional model of nonessential rockets. This cost productivity has opened up valuable open doors for business space investigation, satellite send-offs, and the potential for human missions to Mars.

Musk's vision for space colonization, with Mars as a point of convergence, addresses a drawn out obligation to the endurance and extension of humankind past Earth. While still in the beginning phases, SpaceX's accomplishments have reignited public interest in space investigation, moving another age of researchers, specialists, and space aficionados. The tradition of SpaceX, similar as Tesla, reaches out past its nearby industry influence, impacting worldwide viewpoints on the conceivable outcomes of room travel.

Social Effect and Development Motivation:

Tesla's heritage additionally reaches out to its social effect and its job in moving advancement. Musk's irregular authority style, combined with Tesla's troublesome methodology, has formed public view of business venture and mechanical advancement. Musk's utilization of online entertainment, his eagerness to face challenges, and his capacity to convey a strong vision have added to Tesla's way of life as an automaker as well as a social peculiarity.

Tesla's impact goes past its vehicles; it has pervaded mainstream society and affected conversations on maintainability, innovation, and the fate of transportation. The intense fan base, frequently alluded to as the "Tesla people group," reflects brand steadfastness as well as a common faith in Musk's vision for a practical and mechanically progressed future. Tesla's items, from the unmistakable electric vehicles to energy capacity arrangements, have become images of development and a promise to a cleaner, more manageable world.

The social effect of Tesla reaches out to the more extensive tech industry, rousing business visionaries and new companies to seek after nervy objectives and challenge laid out standards. Musk's readiness to handle apparently impossible difficulties has turned into a guide for the individuals who seek to upset ventures, push the limits of innovation, and add to settling worldwide difficulties.

Difficulties and Reactions:

In spite of the noteworthy progress of Musk's vision and Tesla's enduring heritage, it is fundamental to recognize the difficulties and reactions that go with such aggressive undertakings. Musk's authority style, portrayed by serious workplaces and elevated standards, has confronted investigation. Reports of working environment challenges at Tesla, including high worker turnover and work debates, bring up issues about the harmony among development and representative prosperity. The effect on industry elements remembers expanded consideration for working environment rehearses, with conversations around the moral obligations of pioneers in cultivating solid workplaces.

Administrative examination and lawful difficulties are one more feature of the complicated scene in which Tesla works. Musk's public assertions, especially via online entertainment, have prompted lawful difficulties and administrative examinations.

From SEC examinations to lawful disagreements regarding business choices and public correspondence, Tesla's endeavors have explored a complex legitimate scene. This examination has suggestions for industry elements as controllers evaluate the requirement for oversight and responsibility in areas affected by Musk's endeavors.

Moral contemplations in computerized reasoning (artificial intelligence) additionally become possibly the most important factor, given Musk's association in OpenAI. The discussion over the capable turn of events and sending of man-made intelligence innovations is a huge part of Musk's effect on industry elements. The effect stretches out to conversations about the moral ramifications of cutting edge man-made intelligence frameworks and the requirement for administrative oversight to guarantee the dependable utilization of computerized reasoning.

An Enduring Effect on What's to come

All in all, Elon Musk's vision and Tesla's enduring heritage address an imposing power that has reshaped enterprises, motivated development, and impacted worldwide points of view on innovation and maintainability. Musk's venturesome objectives, from changing the auto area with electric vehicles to pushing the limits of room investigation with SpaceX, have made a permanent imprint on the direction of various businesses.

Tesla's inheritance is diverse, including the change of the car business, the combination of feasible energy arrangements, and the interruption of room investigation standards. The organization's effect stretches out past customary measurements of progress; it has turned into a social peculiarity, motivating another influx of business people, molding public conversations on supportability, and reclassifying assumptions for mechanical development.

As Tesla keeps on exploring difficulties and push the limits of what is reachable, Musk's vision stays a directing power. The continuous improvements in battery innovation, the extension of charging framework, and the quest for completely independent driving capacities are demonstrative of Musk's obligation to a future that embraces supportability, development, and versatility.

While difficulties and reactions are intrinsic chasing after aggressive objectives, they don't lessen the significant effect of Musk's vision and Tesla's inheritance. The social, mechanical, and vast changes put into high gear by Musk's endeavors have expansive ramifications that stretch out past individual organizations. As the world wrestles with worldwide difficulties, for example, environmental change, supportable energy arrangements, and the eventual fate of room investigation, Musk's impact is probably going to persevere, proceeding to shape the direction of enterprises and worldwide points of view in the years to come. The tradition of Musk and Tesla isn't just about the outcome of individual endeavors yet about the persevering through influence on the aggregate creative mind and the determined quest for a future characterized by development and maintainability.

8.2. Looking Ahead: The Future Trajectory of Tesla's Success

Looking forward, the direction of Tesla's prosperity is ready to proceed with its vertical rising, driven by a juncture of elements going from innovative progressions and market elements to Elon Musk's visionary initiative. As Tesla explores the advancing scene of the auto and energy businesses, a few key regions offer bits of knowledge into the future course of the organization.

Electric Vehicle Advancement:

Key to Tesla's future achievement is its proceeded with center around electric vehicle (EV) advancement. The auto business is going through a huge change, with expanding accentuation on supportability and a shift away from conventional gas powered motors. Tesla, with its laid out presence and mechanical ability, is strategically situated to profit by this pattern.

The impending setup of Tesla vehicles, including the Cybertruck, the Tesla Semi, and the reputed conservative vehicle, highlights the organization's obligation to differentiating its contributions. The Cybertruck, with its modern plan and strong capacities, addresses Tesla's introduction to the worthwhile pickup truck market. The Tesla Semi, intended for cargo pulling, expects to upset the business transportation area by furnishing an electric option with significant expense investment funds over conventional diesel trucks.

As well as extending its vehicle setup, Tesla's emphasis on propelling battery innovation is a vital driver of future achievement. The advancement of the 4680 battery cell, declared during Tesla's Battery Day, guarantees higher energy thickness, lower costs, and further developed execution. This innovative jump is indispensable to Musk's vision of making electric vehicles more reasonable and open to a more extensive market.

Independent Driving and Full Self-Driving (FSD) abilities additionally highlight unmistakably in Tesla's future direction. Musk's obligation to accomplishing full independence is reflected in the constant refinement of Tesla's Autopilot framework and the organization of FSD highlights through over-the-air refreshes. The effective execution of FSD can possibly reclassify transportation elements, offering upgraded security as well as opening additional opportunities for shared portability and independent armadas.

Worldwide Extension and Market Infiltration:

Tesla's worldwide extension is an essential support point for its future achievement. While the organization has laid out a huge presence in business sectors like North America, Europe, and China, there is space for additional development. Venture into developing business sectors and districts with expanding interest for electric vehicles is a sensible move toward boost market entrance.

China, specifically, assumes a crucial part in Tesla's worldwide system. The Gigafactory Shanghai, Tesla's most memorable assembling office outside the US, has empowered the organization to take advantage of the world's biggest car market. The progress of the Model 3 in China highlights the potential for Tesla to duplicate its market strength in different areas. As the Chinese government keeps on stressing electric portability and manageable transportation, Tesla's presence is probably going to reinforce further.

Past China, Tesla's entrance into new business sectors, like India, connotes a proactive way to deal with worldwide development. The Indian market, with its developing working class and expanding natural cognizance, presents a chance for Tesla to lay out a traction. Musk's tweet communicating revenue in carrying Tesla to India and the ensuing declaration of an Indian auxiliary demonstrate the organization's essential aim to investigate and gain by developing business sectors.

Framework Improvement and Charging Organization:

The extension of Tesla's Supercharger network is a basic part of its future achievement. As electric vehicle reception develops, the requirement for a hearty and far reaching charging foundation becomes basic. Tesla's exclusive Supercharger organization, known for its speed and unwavering quality, gives the organization an upper hand and addresses a vital worry for potential EV purchasers — range nervousness.

The essential situation of Superchargers along significant travel courses, in metropolitan communities, and at key objections adds to Tesla's strength in charging foundation. Looking forward, the proceeded with extension of the Supercharger organization, both concerning the quantity of stations and the presentation of V4 Superchargers with higher charging limit, lines up with the organization's obligation to giving consistent and advantageous charging encounters for Tesla proprietors.

Besides, Musk's receptiveness to permitting different automakers to utilize the Supercharger organization, gave they adjust to Tesla's charging standard, addresses a likely road for income age and joint effort. This methodology, whenever executed, could situate Tesla as a central participant in electric vehicle fabricating as well as a forerunner in charging framework, encouraging a more cooperative and interoperable electric vehicle biological system.

Energy Arrangements and Maintainable Power Age:

Tesla's introduction to energy arrangements, including sun oriented power age and energy stockpiling, is an essential move that lines up with Musk's vision of a far reaching and reasonable energy biological system. The combination of sun based rooftop tiles, Powerwall, Powerpack, and Megapack positions Tesla as an all encompassing clean energy supplier, tending to transportation as well as more extensive energy challenges.

The versatility of Tesla's energy stockpiling arrangements is a vital consider the organization's future achievement. The far reaching reception of Powerwall for private applications, combined with bigger scope arrangements like Powerpack and Megapack for business and utility-scale projects, adds to network strength, sustainable power coordination, and the decentralization of force age. As the world changes towards cleaner and stronger energy frameworks, Tesla's part in giving versatile energy stockpiling arrangements turns out to be progressively crucial.

Tesla's Energy division is additionally investigating Virtual Power Plants (VPPs) and lattice administrations, permitting Tesla to take part in energy advertises and add to the security of the electrical network. This broadening of contributions upgrades income streams as well as positions Tesla as a central participant in molding the fate of energy dispersion and utilization.

Difficulties and Contemplations:

While the direction of Tesla's prosperity seems promising, it is critical to recognize and address possible difficulties and contemplations that might affect the organization's future.

Market Rivalry:

As the electric vehicle market extends, rivalry is heightening. Conventional automakers, perceiving the shift towards charge, are putting vigorously in creating electric vehicle arrangements. The test for Tesla is to keep up with its administrative role in the midst of expanded rivalry. Separating itself through mechanical development, brand devotion, and a promise to manageability will be critical in holding piece of the pie.

Store network Limitations:

The worldwide store network, set apart by intricacies and weaknesses, represents a gamble to Tesla's creation limit. From semiconductor deficiencies to unrefined substance acquisition challenges, disturbances in the store network can affect fabricating timetables and item accessibility. Broadening of providers, vital amassing of basic parts, and coordinated inventory network the board are techniques Tesla might utilize to relieve such dangers.

Administrative Climate:

The administrative scene, both regarding auto norms and natural strategies, is liable to change. Advancing guidelines, especially in locales critical to Tesla's market, can affect fabricating processes, vehicle certificates, and consistence necessities. Pro-active commitment with policymakers and an adaptable way to deal with adjusting to administrative changes will be fundamental for Tesla's supported achievement.

Public Insight and Notoriety:

Tesla's prosperity is unpredictably attached to public discernment and brand no-toriety. High-profile episodes, administrative examination, or contentions connected with working environment practices can impact general assessment.

Keeping up with straightforwardness, tending to worries quickly, and building up Tesla's obligation to manageability and development are basic parts in safeguarding and improving the organization's standing.

Innovative Dangers and Online protection:

As Tesla keeps on improving, the combination of cutting edge innovations, espe-cially in independent driving, presents new dangers. Network protection dangers, possible mechanical disappointments, or public episodes including independent vehi-cles can influence buyer trust and administrative acknowledgment. Powerful network protection measures, thorough testing conventions, and clear correspondence on the limits of advancing innovations are basic to moderate such dangers.

Decision: A Future Characterized by Vision and Development

All in all, the future direction of Tesla's prosperity is formed by a mix of visionary authority, mechanical development, vital extension, and a pledge to manageability. Elon Musk's brassy vision, from reforming transportation with electric vehicles to building an exhaustive clean energy biological system, keeps on directing the organiza-tion towards new wildernesses.

As Tesla explores the difficulties and valuable open doors ahead, its job in affecting the auto, energy, and innovation areas is probably going to develop. The organization's prosperity goes past monetary measurements; it addresses an extraordinary power that has re-imagined businesses, enlivened worldwide discussions on manageability, and set new principles for mechanical development.

The proceeded with center around electric vehicle advancement, worldwide ex-tension, foundation improvement, energy arrangements, and addressing potential difficulties mirrors Tesla's dynamic way to deal with molding what's to come. Musk's capacity to turn, adjust, and drive development highlights the strength of Tesla's vision in a quickly evolving scene.

As the world changes towards a more economical and mechanically progressed future, Tesla's job as a trailblazer and pioneer is probably going to endure. The organization's impact reaches out past individual items; it envelops a social shift towards embracing clean energy, reexamining transportation standards, and testing the customary way of thinking.

At last, the future direction of Tesla's prosperity isn't just about creating electric vehicles or creating energy stockpiling arrangements; it is tied in with adding to a more extensive cultural change. The tradition of Elon Musk and Tesla lies in the items they make as well as in the expanding influences of their vision — rousing businesses, encouraging development, and molding a future where manageability and innovation mix to rethink what is conceivable. As the excursion unfurls, Tesla's effect on the world isn't just estimated in miles driven or kilowatt-hours put away; it is estimated in the changes in outlook, discussions ignited, and the aggregate creative mind reshaped by a dream that arrives at into the great beyond.